The Practitioner Inquiry Series

Marilyn Cochran-Smith and Susan L. Lytle, *SERIES EDITORS*

Interpreting Teacher Practice:
Two Continuing Stories
RENATE SCHULZ

Creating Democratic Classrooms:
The Struggle to Integrate Theory and Practice
LANDON E. BEYER, Editor

D0141156

Interpreting Teacher Practice ... Two Continuing Stories

RENATE SCHULZ

Foreword by D. Jean Clandinin

TEACHERS
COLLEGE
PRESS

Teachers College
Columbia University
New York and London

Published by Teachers College Press, 1234 Amsterdam Avenue, New York, NY 10027

Library of Congress Cataloging-in-Publication Data

Schulz, Renate.
    Interpreting teacher practice : two continuing stories / Renate Schulz : foreword by D. Jean Clandinin.
        p.   cm. — (The practitioner inquiry series)
    Includes bibliographical references (p.   ) and index.
    ISBN 0-8077-3559-0 (cloth). — ISBN 0-8077-3558-2 (pbk.)
        1. Teachers—Canada—Case studies. 2. English teachers—Canada—Case studies. 3. Teaching—Canada—Case studies. 4. Action research in education—Canada—Case studies.   I. Title.
    II. Series.
    LB1775.4.C2S38   1997
    371.1′02—dc20   96-30690

ISBN 0-8077-3558-2 (paper)
ISBN 0-8077-3559-0 (cloth)

Printed on acid-free paper
Manufactured in the United States of America

03 02 01 00 99 98 97 96   8 7 6 5 4 3 2 1

Contents

Foreword

It is a sunshine-filled warm spring afternoon as I finish reading Renate's book. I gaze out at the river valley, at trees barely tinged green with the promise of spring. I decide to go for a walk for I feel unease, a sense of having read a "writerly text," a text designed to "disrupt our settled expectations" (p. 137). I pull my anorak on and head toward the river, hoping the water, muddied by spring run-off, will help me name the unease. For how can I feel such unease when I feel resonance with Renate's lines, lines like,

> Collaborative narrative inquiry is one such new way of doing research. It redefines the relationship between researcher and researched and provides a structure for telling teachers' stories within a framework of care. It becomes our responsibility, then, to consider how we will read these stories. By repositioning ourselves in relation to the text and adopting a participatory stance, our reading becomes more consonant with the principles and methods of collaborative narrative inquiry. (p. 141)

As the river swirls by, sweeping up branches, leaves, and other bits of debris, I realize I have been swept into the stories in Renate's book. Her stories make compelling reading for me. They sweep me in and yet, even as I am swept along, caught in the drama of evolving researcher-participant relationships, I realize that I am unsettled. And I find myself caught in my need to order my knowing in the process of telling stories. I, as Renate points out, have done my reading "from within a situated world." I search back to coming to know Renate.

I first met Renate sometime early in her process of trying to negotiate her accounts with Raymond and James. She had already written her accounts, accounts largely written as if she were "on a mountain top viewing and recording the scene below, from a privileged vantage point." Raymond's response, at least in my telling of Renate's story, seemed to awaken her to her practice as a researcher. And, in the pages of this book, Renate makes her own evolving story as researcher painfully clear. As I realize this, I begin to understand my unease.

I realize I had come to the book with expectations that I would learn mostly about two teachers who participated in a research study with Renate, a research study that has raised many issues about the nature of collaborative research and the relationships between researcher and participant in the field, about the construction of field texts and the representation of those field texts in a research text. I expected to read of "the struggles and tensions of the classroom" (p. 123) and expected to "interpret and draw conclusions" (p. 123). I felt I was settled knowing my reader's role as one of "interrogating the text in order to understand the partiality and managed nature of the narrative" (p. 124).

As Renate tells us, in reading narrative inquiry we encounter "not just a text, but a real person within the lived story of the narrative inquiry" (p. 138). I was ready to encounter James and Raymond and I realized I had unexpectedly encountered Renate, who tells us a story of herself as researcher growing into the complexity of what it means to engage in collaborative narrative inquiry. Her story is powerful for she does not shy away from the tensions, the uncertainties, the pain she encounters in having her research text first given back by Raymond. Instead she tells us how she used that moment as the beginning of her inquiry, of her restorying again and again until she can name what she has come to know about what it means to live a life as collaborative narrative inquirer. She ends by saying "the narrative line of this story does not lead to closure; to a problem resolved." In telling her research story, Renate leads us to consider how not only teachers like Raymond and James are learning to restory and change their practices, but how she, as researcher, is learning to story and restory her practices. In that, it is a story to live by, and one that will guide me in my own process of learning to restory my research practices.

D. Jean Clandinin,
University of Alberta

Acknowledgments

With grateful thanks I acknowledge the two teachers whose stories are central to this book. Charles Moody and "Raymond" opened their classrooms to me, shared their thoughts with me, and gave many hours of their time to this project.

Jean Clandinin's and Nel Noddings' influence is strongly evident in this book. I thank them for their wonderful writing, for their thoughtful reading of my early drafts, and for their encouraging comments.

Special thanks go to colleagues Charlotte Reid and Kathie Webb for their careful reading of the manuscript and for the generosity of their response.

I am grateful to Brian Ellerbeck of Teachers College Press and to Sarah Biondello for her work in editing this manuscript.

Jill Wharton deserves special acknowledgment. Quietly and efficiently, she transformed page after page of longhand into an error-free finished copy, doing all this during her spare time because she likes to keep busy. Thank you, Jill.

Most of all, my love and thanks go to three very special people: my husband, Bill, and my children, Jennifer and Brendan—for their unfailing encouragement and support.

Interpreting Teacher Practice ... Two Continuing Stories

Chapter 1

Beginning with Stories

*When a day passes it is no longer there. What remains of it? Nothing
more than a story. If stories weren't told or books weren't written,
man would live like the beasts, only for the day. Today, we live, but
by tomorrow today will be a story. The whole world, all human life, is
one long story.*

Singer (1976, pp. 10–11)

Teaching is a complex activity, and although abundant research has
been done to examine the nature of teaching, it is still far from being
fully understood. The mystery of what really happens in the classroom,
why and how it happens, continues to challenge us. Teaching is a
uniquely personal and intuitive activity that requires us to focus on its
qualitative nature if we are to increase our understanding of it. Research
that focuses on the personal and recognizes the importance of the autobiographical in the process of teaching, while at the same time chronicling the classroom actions of the teacher, provides a broad evidential
base from which to draw conclusions about the practice of teaching.

Clandinin and Connelly (1994), writing about the study of narrative
and storytelling as a way of coming to know about teachers and teaching, tell us that "people by nature lead storied lives and tell stories of
those lives, whereas narrative researchers describe such lives, collect
and tell stories of them, and write narratives of experience" (p. 416).
Research that is founded on teachers' stories conveys a reality in a way
that no theoretical formulation can, because storytelling is at the heart
of human conduct. Britton (1982) tells us that "our memories of past
experiences are in story form, are narratives. We so readily construct
stories out of our past experiences that it is difficult to perceive that
anything has been 'constructed' at all" (p. 153). The structure of the
stories we tell, their narrative line, gives form to our ideas and meanings. Telling stories is an activity that orders meaning, and in this way,
narrative discourse contributes to knowing. The equating of narrating
and knowing also has support from philological analyses. *Know* and
narrate have a common origin in the Indo-European *gna*. To know and

to narrate, therefore, are intimately related human actions. Connelly and Clandinin (1988) write that:

> the narratives of all of us are complex and contain various threads that knit a kind of continuity and unity in our professional lives . . . they are particular orderings of prior experience, brought to bear on new situations. As such these orderings yield new ways of telling a story of who we are and how it is that we are doing what we are doing. (p. 153)

The collection of classroom data and their biographical underpinnings—those personal, historical, and professional experiences that influence the routines, patterns, and habits of teachers—is a relatively new method in the study of teaching. Biographical stories are collected as explanatory material, recovered as various narrative unities are traced, so that the teachers' stories can be told with new meaning. Connelly and Clandinin (1990) write that the stories "function as arguments in which we learn something essentially human by understanding an actual life or community as lived" (p. 8).

Narrative inquiry as a research method is gaining increasing recognition as a powerful way of coming to know and understand the lives of teachers and the complex nature of teaching. Although much is being learned through narrative inquiry, more needs to be understood about the process, about the forums within which we tell stories of teaching, the manner in which these stories are received and recorded, and, once recorded, the different ways in which the texts of teachers' stories can be read.

The following chapters contain the story of a long-term research project conducted with two high school English teachers in Canada. An analysis of the stories and the practices of these teachers revealed the complex interplay of biography, beliefs, and teacher practice, and illustrated the enormous power of the past to inform and shape their professional development. At the same time, the study illustrated the complexity of the process of change, as well as the deceiving face of change. The first four chapters of this book are devoted to this part of the story.

After one full school year as an observer-participant in the classrooms of the two teachers and another year devoted to continued conversations with the teachers while writing the final report, completing the research report in the third year of the project signaled for me the end of the venture. That was, however, not to be the case. What followed attests to the ongoing nature of qualitative research.

Raymond, one of the teachers in the project, was dismayed at the portrait of his teaching self that he saw in the pages of the final report. His anguish and dismay prompted me to return to the project to take a critical and retrospective look at the process we had engaged in. In the process of examining what we had done and how we might have done things differently, Raymond and I began to question the nature of our research relationship. Ours had been a collegial partnership, but we soon began to understand how things might have happened differently if instead our research had been collaborative. Chapter Five is devoted to an examination of our research relationship and the ethical issues we faced within that relationship. The chapter explores the kind of ethical issues that arise within a research context where we work closely with teachers over a long period of time. The ethical issues are reframed and placed within the context of a collaborative inquiry as Connelly and Clandinin (1988, 1990) define it and then viewed from the perspective of an ethic of caring as Noddings (1984, 1987, 1991, 1992) describes it.

Questions and possibilities about new ways of working together and coming to know about teachers and teaching led us next to an examination of the texts of teachers' stories. The texts of teachers' stories have not been made public until recently. We do not have a long tradition of listening to teachers' voices or reading teachers' stories as a way of gaining insight into the complexities of the classroom. We are, in fact, new readers of teachers' stories. Yet for the most part, our reading habits are rooted in old notions of the role of the author, the function of the text, and the purpose of reading. From the perspective of contemporary literary theory, successful reading of a text depends very much on the extent to which a text can activate the individual reader's faculties of perceiving and processing. Thus the way in which the text is perceived depends as much on the reader as on the text. What do we as researchers and readers bring to our reading of the classroom as text and to the texts of teacher narratives? As writers of research we start with blank pages and compose upon them a meaningful text. As readers we start with an already written text and compose an interpreted meaning.

The final chapter of this book addresses this interrelationship of writing and reading and the attendant issue of voice. Whose voice is in the text, and what voice does the reader give to a text? The field of literary criticism can help us to address these questions. By drawing on the work of reading theorists and critical literary theorists, we can extend our understanding of the ways in which we read narrative research texts, interpret them, ascribe meaning to them, and learn from them.

Eisner (1984) provides the directive from which we can trace the story of our research project forward from its point of origin:

If educational research is to inform educational practice, researchers will have to go back to the schools for a fresh look at what is going on there. We will have to develop a language that is relevant to educational practice, one that does justice to teaching and learning in educational settings, and we will need to develop methods of inquiry that do not squeeze the educational life out of what we study in such settings. (p. 451)

To go back to the schools and work with teachers in order to try to gain a greater understanding of the practice of teaching was my goal as I began to work with two high school English teachers. James and Raymond taught in the same city but in different schools. They had very different teaching styles, but both were very experienced, each having taught for over 20 years. I was interested in examining good teaching practices in secondary school English classrooms, and had chosen Raymond and James because of their established reputations. I began my work shortly after a new Language Arts curriculum had been introduced in the schools. The new curriculum called for a shift from a teacher-centered to a student-centered classroom approach, with emphasis placed on language and the transaction of knowledge, as opposed to the emphasis in the old curriculum, which had been on literature and the transmission of knowledge. Response to this new curriculum had been varied. Its merits were strongly debated by teachers. Many teachers, used to a literature-based curriculum, could not understand and therefore did not endorse the new focus on language, the emphasis on oracy, on group work, on process, and on student-centered learning. James' and Raymond's individual responses to these demands for change in classroom practice immediately became the starting point of our conversations.

When I contacted Raymond for the first time shortly after school began in the fall, I explained my interest in studying good teaching practices and asked permission to become an observer-participant in his classroom for what I initially assumed would be a period of a few months. Raymond agreed to my request immediately, almost eagerly. Delight, excitement, and anticipation were all evident in the tone of his voice as he told me on the telephone that he was used to having visitors in his classroom, that I was welcome to come whenever and as often as I wished, and that he would make the necessary arrangements with the principal to have my visits approved.

When I called James to explain my study and request permission to be an observer-participant in his classroom, he listened quietly, but reserved his decision until we had an opportunity to meet and discuss my proposal in more detail. Over coffee a few days later, I explained the reason for my study, how I would go about collecting the data, and what purpose my observations might eventually serve. James received my explanations politely but expressed some uneasiness about being observed in the classroom.

While Raymond had welcomed the student-centered, language-based, process-oriented focus of the new curriculum, James had not. Raymond explained to me that his teaching style had been undergoing a tremendous change process over the last few years and that he welcomed the new curriculum because it reflected so well his new beliefs about teaching. Not only did he embrace this new curriculum, he also became a spokesperson for it. He conducted workshops and opened his classroom door to teachers who wanted to learn about the teaching method of this new curriculum.

James, however, rejected the dictates of the new curriculum. He described himself as traditional, literature-based, and teacher-centered. He saw these characteristics as part of his personal teaching style, and dismissed suggestions for change in his teaching practice. He felt that the way he taught, although it was, in his words, old-fashioned, "was nevertheless successful and effective." Not only did he continue to teach in a teacher-centered fashion as he always had, he made his views known by publishing in local professional journals. In one such article, after arguing that just as different students have different learning styles, different teachers should be allowed their different teaching styles, James charged that the implementation of the new curriculum was taking on Orwellian overtones:

> Alternative programs are viewed with distrust; "traditional" teachers with suspicion. We are being subjected to regular propaganda extolling the virtues of the new way. We are given five-year plans and constant reminders of the quotas to be met. The teacher who won't integrate is the object of scorn. He's not running in all four modes, we say. Principals have been given directives to ensure that the new curriculum is being taught. Recently, in my division, we were asked to give an account of ourselves. Was this simply a request for information? Or was pressure being applied to bring renegades into line? Will some of us be labelled "suspect" and worthy of further watching? When will the Curriculum Police come knocking on my classroom door?

Not surprisingly, I felt that James might view me as the Curriculum Police. I sensed his reluctance to have me in the classroom, but at the same time, his integrity as a professional seemed to compel him to invite me, for as he said, if he was "going to make rumblings about the new curriculum,'' he had better be prepared to allow someone to come into his classroom in order to observe him.

When I began my weekly visits to the schools I was conscious of the need to establish rapport and to gain the respect of both teachers. In addition, I was especially sensitive to James' comfort level as I became part of his classroom. His hesitance to have me in the classroom stood in sharp contrast to Raymond's open welcome. But in an unexpected turn of events, Raymond, who was so at ease with visitors to his classroom, told me during my second visit that he felt a sense of nervousness about my presence. He had wondered whether he should change his lesson plans on the days when I was there, but then decided to proceed as usual. I assured him that that was what I wanted.

As we stood around the coffee machine in the staff room, I confessed to Raymond that I was also feeling unsure about my role in the classroom and uncomfortable about possibly imposing on his time. He gave an almost audible sigh of relief when I explained this, and he said that this made him feel better. I sensed that our relationship was shifting to new, more equal ground. I was less threatening now as the outsider from the university with expert status. I too had my uncertainties about launching into this new project, which was to be a learning experience for all of us.

Initially, I merely observed in the classroom, asking few questions and waiting for indications from the teachers before initiating discussions. I hoped that over time I would become accepted, and that this acceptance would lead to a productive collaborative relationship in which I could freely question, probe, and share thoughts with both Raymond and James. Almost always, right from the beginning, spontaneous conversations developed after the end of classes. At first the focus of these conversations centered only on what had happened in the lessons, and how we thought and felt about the classes. As always, relationships change over time, and the changes in our conversations reflected the increasing familiarity between us. Our after-class conversations began to last longer and to reach beyond the happenings of the day. The questions we asked of each other and our conversations led us into tentative explorations of various aspects of James' and Raymond's practices. They talked about their frustrations in teaching, their hopes, their successes and failures, their beliefs, their plans, and their pasts. Suddenly, almost surprisingly, we found ourselves facing a direction that I had not envisioned at the start of the project. We began to focus on the way in which the teachers' pasts functioned as a prelude to their present teaching practices. We began to tell stories of the past. We talked about how we had entered the teaching profession, about those who had influenced us, and about the experiences that had shaped our beliefs about teaching.

Raymond was particularly excited about exploring the role that the past played in his development as a teacher. He commented frequently that as a new teacher he had been strongly influenced by his past, that he had worked hard to separate himself from that past, and that consequently he was now very different, both as a person and as a teacher. He wanted very much to investigate the process of this change.

We discussed the new direction that our conversations were taking and agreed to make it the focus of our inquiry. Then we renegotiated my stay in the teachers' classrooms, and I received administrative permission to remain for the whole school year. The stories and events that unfolded thereafter were not what I could have predicted at the beginning of our project.

Having decided to focus our inquiry on the interplay of biography, beliefs, and teacher practice, Raymond began to step up the pace of the study. He urged me to come to his class more often, and suggested additional meeting times so that our conversations could be both uninterrupted and longer. James too called and invited me for additional class visits when students were going to be doing things that he thought I might enjoy being a part of. Although it had taken James longer to feel at ease with me, after working together for several months we were very comfortable in each other's presence and his frequent invitations of ''let's get a coffee'' always signaled a time for us to talk.

In addition to the spontaneous conversations that took place in the classroom, in the hallways, or in the staff room, we also scheduled specific interview times. Each teacher was interviewed for a total of approximately sixteen hours. These interviews took place in my home or in a restaurant over lunch, and continued through the writing-up of the research. I hoped that the comfortable and relaxed atmosphere in front of the fireplace in my home, or over lunch in a restaurant, would contribute to the quality of the information we shared during these sessions, and indeed it did. Both teachers spoke of the isolation of the classroom and the fact that they had very few opportunities to discuss their teaching. Although many teachers visited Raymond's classroom to learn about his teaching methods, these visits were always brief. He seldom, if ever, had the opportunity for sustained discussions of his teaching practice and beliefs. Our conversations gave both teachers that opportunity. The measure of familiarity, comfort, and trust between us was now such that we could challenge each other's assumptions and assertions, so that our discussions during these interviews were rich and informative. Throughout, the interviews retained the quality of conversations, which were not formally terminated at the end of a session, but rather remained suspended until the next time we met for another interesting and lively conversational encounter.

I audiotaped only a few of these conversations with Raymond, and made notes on the others. James asked not to have any of our conversations taped, and I honored that request. At approximately six-to-eight-week intervals both teachers received copies of the accumulated field-notes. These notes included the happenings in the classroom, direct quotations of the conversations of both teachers and students, and the points of discussion in our conversations, as well as my own thoughts on all these occurrences. James and Raymond were invited to corroborate my observations and elaborate on, explain, correct, or comment on any aspect of this chronicle of our conversations and classroom activities. I was able to use this same compilation of fieldnotes to reflect on the meaning of familiar and unfamiliar events, and to weigh my thoughts about classroom activities against the writings of others. At the same time, the writings of critics, philosophers, and educators continued to shape my reflections, focus my observations, and inform my thinking as I worked with and wrote James' and Raymond's stories.

Like a text, the stories of James and Raymond that follow invite attentive readings. The stories invite us to see patterns and connections that are the starting places for understanding and interpretation. Texts, as Umberto Eco (1979) points out, "are lazy machineries that ask someone to do part of their job" (p. 214). But the term "texts" does not refer only to books. Textual studies have pushed beyond the boundaries of pages and books into society and culture, into institutional practices and social structures that can themselves be compared to genres, and studied as codes and texts. The empirical tradition that endorsed unified readings of presumably stable texts has given way to new theories of textuality that have produced tremendous shifts in the way we read and understand texts. We have a better appreciation now of the transactional nature of reading and of our role as meaning-makers in the act of reading. Iser (1978) writes that the successful reading of a text:

> depends on the extent to which the text can activate the individual reader's faculties of perceiving and processing. . . . Of course, the text is a "structured prefigurement," but that which is given has to be received, and the way in which it is received depends as much on the reader as on the text. (p. 107)

As English teachers, both Raymond and James live with stories. They read stories, study stories, interpret stories, and teach stories. But these are always the stories of others. The following chapters are a telling of some of James' and Raymond's stories. They are but one telling, and at that only a partial one, for as Margaret Atwood (1985) writes:

> It's impossible to say a thing exactly the way it was, because what you say can never be exact, you always have to leave something out, there are too many parts, sides, crosscurrents, nuances. (p. 126)

Nevertheless, James' and Raymond's stories are an opportunity for others to see what I saw as I read the texts of their classroom practice and recorded their lived and told stories. The texts of their stories are also an invitation for others to see and read differently, for the power of stories lies in their perpetual openness to further interpretation. Other interpretations create the possibility for us to understand in a new way, to see in a new way, to rethink the views we hold, and to make new meanings.

Chapter 2

James' Story

"Read slowly and deliberately," James directs a student in his twelfth-grade English class as she prepares to read Shakespeare's sonnet CXVI, "Let me not to the marriage of true minds." "Linger over every word," he counsels. She completes her reading, and after a second reading of the poem, the class talks about what love is, about the form of the poem, the quatrains, the couplet, the tone change, and how the form is appropriate for the meaning of the poem. Then James encourages the class to read the poem "as often as you like. Linger over those words. Get an image of the storm-tossed ship."

The next poem is one of James' favorite Shakespearean sonnets.

LXXIII.

That time of year thou mayst in me behold
When yellow leaves, or none, or few, do hang
Upon those boughs which shake against the cold,
Bare ruin'd choirs, where late the sweet birds sang.

In me thou see'st the twilight of such day
As after sunset fadeth in the west,
Which by and by black night doth take away,
Death's second self, that seals up all in rest.

In me thou see'st the glowing of such fire
That on the ashes of his youth doth lie,
As the death-bed whereon it must expire
Consumed with that which it was nourish'd by.

This thou perceivest, which makes thy love more strong,
To love that well which thou must leave ere long.

Again he begins with a reading, and then the class talks about the form. "Each quatrain is a little unit," James tells the class, and then asks, "How is it obvious that each quatrain is different?" One student suggests that different seasons are depicted in each quatrain, and James replies, "No, there are different images in each. Let's do it again. Quatrain by quatrain." A different student is asked to read each section,

and then James begins with the first quatrain and talks about the cycle
of the seasons. The class is familiar with *Macbeth*, having studied it in
the eleventh grade, and so he connects the "yellow leaves" of the sonnet to Macbeth's mention of the "yellow leaf." He quotes Macbeth's
"To-morrow, and to-morrow, and to-morrow" speech, talks about the
autumn of life, recites Macbeth's lines—"I have lived long enough: my
way of life is fall'n into the sear"—and explains that this is the time of
life when you look back. Then James asks the students what images
they see in the second and third quatrains, and together they explore
the figures of sunset, twilight, and expiring fire. "The couplet is an
enigma," James announces, and then asks the class to define that term.
To provide a clue for his students, and a context for the word, he tells
them that Hamlet is an enigma, and one student responds with the
suggestion that "enigma" means an "intellectual" or a "thinker."
Since this is not correct, James offers further help and explains to the
class the circumstances surrounding the composition of Elgar's "Enigma Variations." Finally the students recognize that an enigma is a
"mystery" or a "puzzle," and they turn their attention to puzzling out
the meaning of the line "To love that well which thou must leave ere
long." One student suggests that this line means, "He's dying and she
might be leaving," while another says that "Maybe she's dying, too,
because as his wife, she'd be as old as he." After explaining his interpretation of the couplet and entertaining several other possibilities for the
meaning of this line, James suggests they read the sonnet again. One
student is asked to read the first quatrain, while the rest of the class is
directed to close their eyes and visualize the scene of the first section.
James tells his students to "concentrate on the imagery, the word pictures. What are you seeing?" For some, the most vivid images of the
first quatrain are the trees, while others visualize the wind blowing, the
choir, or the church. James explains that structurally, cathedrals were
built in a cross-shaped form. He draws a diagram on the board and tells
the class that the part of the cathedral where the service is said is called
the choir. He asks if anyone has visited a cathedral, and one of the
students, who had been on a choir tour to England, comes forward to
add a few more details to the diagram on the board, to explain where
the pipe organ would be located and the choir situated. James then
draws the students' attention to the resemblance between the vaulting
of a Gothic aisle and an avenue of trees whose upper branches meet to
form an arch overhead. He asks the class to "feel" the cold wind and to
visualize the solemn, striking picture of the leafless boughs of the
arched avenue of trees set against the ruined and shattered roof of the
cathedral. The students had already visualized the trees, the blowing

wind, the cathedral, and the choir. James extends and enriches that vision by evoking an even more desolate image through this comparison of the ruined choir of the cathedral with the avenue of leafless trees. He ends by saying, "I think it's my favorite sonnet because of the imagery. A wonderful sonnet. It might be worth memorizing."

The language of literature, its power and its beauty, is for James the focus in his teaching of English. And Shakespeare is one of his favorite authors to teach. When he introduced Shakespeare to the class at the beginning of the year, James stressed that one of the reasons Shakespeare is still studied today is because of the wealth and beauty of the language. Then he handed out a brief article that outlined for the class the many ways in which Shakespeare's language affects our speech even today. Well-known quotations from Shakespeare, Wordsworth, Coleridge, Keats, and Orwell line one wall of his classroom, and James concedes that Orwell's essays on language have had a strong influence on him. Orwell, in his fight against bad English, advocated the precise and accurate use of language. James also instructs his students to be aware of language, to "write simply and clearly, avoiding jargon, circumlocution, and convoluted structures." And he follows his own advice. There is precision both in James' writing and in his speech. He chooses his words with care. At one point, while talking to the class about the comparison in Shakespeare's sonnet of the ruined choir of the cathedral with an avenue of leafless trees, James says, "It's a wonderful collage of images." Then he corrects himself, saying, "No, it's a montage."

James uses every opportunity in class to draw his students' attention to the language of literature, the meaning of words, their derivations, and their effective usage. One student in a tenth-grade class studying *Julius Caesar* suggests that Antony is an egotist. James asks the student whether he thinks Antony is an "egotist" or an "egoist." "What's the difference?" James asks. "What's the French word for egoist?" The student replies, "*égoiste*," and James goes on to explain the difference between "egoist" and "egotist." On another occasion, in a twelfth-grade Milton class, James asks his students, "What do we get from Lethe?", and they respond with "lethargy" and "lethal." In a tenth-grade class again, during a discussion of the word "left," James refers to the denotative and connotative meanings of "right" and "left," "*gauche*" and "*droit*." Then he extends the discussion to include possible similarities in the German use of the word, concludes with the Latin use of the word, and explains the meaning of "sinister," "dexter/ity," and "ambidextrous."

"Latin was always my favorite subject," James says, "and I still

consider it far and away the most useful thing I learned at school."
James began his study of Latin in a private boarding school in Perth,
Australia, a school modeled very much along the lines of English boarding schools, where headmasters ruled, and cricket, rowing, and caning
were practiced. He remembers his school years as somewhat unhappy
times. "Sad as it seems," he says, "when I look back, I don't think any
of them [the teachers] took much interest in me at all." There was one
teacher, however, in whom James took a great deal of interest. That was
Patrick McGushin, the Latin teacher. James remembers his Latin teacher
as "blunt, abrupt, unpredictable, histrionic, likely to fly into a calculated
rage if a boy hadn't done his homework." He remembers being seized
by the hair as a youngster and rocked back and forth as he declined his
Latin nouns: "*Mensa, mensam, mensae, mensae, mensa . . . mensae, men-
sas, mensarum, mensis, mensis.* Patrick McGushin was tough, and as
younger boys we were somewhat afraid of him. And yet, we once did
an elaborate survey of all the students in the class to determine our most
popular teacher, and he was one short of being the unanimous choice.

"I can see him now," James continues, "sitting at his teacher's
desk bouncing a tennis ball up and down and singing 'Come into the
garden, Maud.' It's lamentable that we don't have the crazy characters
anymore. There's educational value in them." "When I think about it,"
James says, "Patrick McGushin influenced me more than I realized, not
to become a teacher, I don't think, but to emulate his rather eccentric
personality, or to create one of my own. One of the reasons I'm a
teacher is because I'm introverted, and teaching is a chance for me to
manifest myself in a situation in a way in which I usually can't or
don't. There is some truth in Shaw's famous dictum about teachers. The
teacher is perhaps the artist manque, who while lacking the creativity of
the artist can at least express himself in his teaching. Like the actor, he
performs in front of his audience.

"I have long suspected that the teacher may develop a different
persona in front of the class. This is perhaps why many of us are ner-
vous when other adults come to observe us. We may have taken on a
different identity. With a captive audience behind the closed door the
teacher is able to develop his own personality and perhaps compensate
for inadequacies in his adult self. Some might even develop an alter ego
in their teacher persona. I am a rather shy person in a group, and don't
contribute much to the conversation. In the classroom I talk a lot. With
students I'm more extroverted; I can perform, recite passages, and play
the eccentric. And I play the eccentric partly because if one can seem
different to the kids, they're more likely to remember. Crazy things
stick. If you're dull and straight you won't be remembered either."

James believes that he remembers the details from his school days "because of their vivid associations," and he continues, "I sometimes stand across the desks to explain the image in 'Why man he doth bestride the narrow world like a Colossus'—for the same reason." He studied Latin with Patrick McGushin for seven years, and as James suggests, "it would be surprising if he hadn't had an influence on me."

Another vivid recollection from James' school days is of being publicly reprimanded by the headmaster during a school assembly, on two occasions several years apart. He was reprimanded for the insolent expression on his face, when in fact he had only been innocently daydreaming. "The memory still hurts," James says. "That experience has influenced my own teaching." And indeed, he often quotes the line from Wordsworth—"little, nameless, unremembered acts/of kindness and of love"—to explain his own patience with students, his willingness to give them the benefit of the doubt, and the seemingly countless make-up opportunities he gives students for incomplete work.

But James recalls one particular incident in his own teaching career when he momentarily forgot how hurtful a teacher's thoughtless actions can be. The memory of this incident is painful even today. He still regrets his actions. His voice catches and he turns his face aside as he begins to tell the story. He was a coach for his school's "Reach for the Top" team. "Reach for the Top" was a televised competition in which teams from various schools competed against each other for speed and accuracy in answering questions drawn from various subject areas. Winning teams then moved on to compete at a regional and national level, and were eligible to win sizeable scholarships as prizes. During the years when this was a popular television program, having a Reach for the Top team in the school, and especially a winning team, was quite prestigious. As the coach of such a team, James made the decision shortly before the competition was televised to replace one of his team members with another student, one who, he thought, was more likely to assure the team a win. The girl who lost her spot on the team was devastated, and the humiliation she felt was painful not only for her, but also for her whole family. In retrospect, James says that he can only imagine the damage he did to her and her family. All the relatives had been invited to the girl's home to watch the match on television, and then she wasn't even a part of the team. James confessed, "I was thinking more of my role as coach and the prestige of winning, and let that overrule my thinking. I would never do that now."

When he remembers his own school days, he recalls that he didn't participate in many things. He supposed that he didn't have the initiative to join the extracurricular activities, and now regrets all those missed opportunities of schooling. He wishes that someone had taken an interest in him, that someone had noticed him and encouraged him to join the band or some other activity—but no one did. Now James does the encouraging, and he notices those students on the borderline, those who need a push. He tells me about one student, a girl who is "brilliant; the writing in her journal is so succinct." She is a troubled girl who has run away from home and has attempted suicide. She doesn't care about school, but James says, "I have to do everything to be sure she passes with an A." He speaks of her brilliance again, her gift for poetry, her understanding and perception, which he says are far greater than his. He feels that she has to become a writer, that he can't let her fail just because she doesn't come to class and doesn't care. He notices her as he would have wanted to be noticed, and because he hopes it will help, he overlooks things and stretches the rules for her.

Brenda is another student James has been concerned about. She is the only native student in his tenth-grade class, and he recognized that she was painfully shy, but was never quite sure how he should handle this. Should he ask her questions in class or not? Would he embarrass her if he asked and she didn't know the answer? What would make her feel most comfortable? One day she started her journal by saying that she was going to write about something serious, and she related how her father had been murdered on the reserve, and how she felt responsible for this. Her journal entry tells of an evening when Brenda went out with her friends and came upon her father, who was drinking with others. He asked Brenda to take him home, but she and her friends had made other arrangements and so she refused. She left. He stayed behind, became involved in a fight, and was killed. Understandably, Brenda felt responsible for his death. Within the pages of her journal, teacher and student were able to talk about what had happened and to talk about Brenda's pain. In responding to another of her entries, James asked Brenda how her school year had been, and hoped that she would be coming back the following year. In her subsequent reply to James, Brenda explained in her journal that although she had had a very good year, and everyone had been very nice to her, she would not be coming back to school in the fall. Because of lack of funds, she and her mother would be returning to the reserve. James was concerned, made some inquiries on Brenda's behalf, and turned to the school counselor for help. Together they were able to make the necessary arrangements so that Brenda could return the following year. She is back in school, still very quiet and shy, and James still worries because he is not sure how to handle her. He noticed that Brenda's assigned extra reading consisted only of popular romance literature, and so he introduced her to *The*

Hobbit. She enjoyed it and so he followed that up by giving her *Lord of the Rings* to read. Now he is agonizing about whether he should give her *April Raintree* next. This is a short but very moving novel about two Métis (mixed-race) sisters and the harsh reality of their life in a city in an alien culture. Brenda is very young, very unaware of native rights movements, and James isn't sure what her reaction will be to the book or whether she is ready for it.

There is a gentleness in the way that James relates to his students, and a patience. He is always ready to make extra efforts for those students who are willing to work, for those who want to learn, and for those who are on the borderline and need an extra nudge. But he explains that he is not so idealistic as to spend time on those who have a negative attitude and do not want to be helped. Although he recognizes that this negative attitude is a cry for help in itself, he does not feel that he can respond to it. It requires more energy, more time, and more effort than he is able to give as a teacher.

When he thinks about teaching and about becoming a teacher, James says, "I can't say that I ever made a conscious decision to enter the teaching profession. I just drifted in from the streets, so to speak. I had almost finished a degree in geology, but after one summer down a mine and another in the bush, I decided that this was not the life for me. On a whim, I knocked on the door of the teacher recruitment office for the state of Western Australia. Somewhat impoverished, I was attracted by a government offer to pay the way of teachers in training. I filled in the forms and gave them to the interviewer. 'Do you have references with you?' he asked.

" 'No,' said I.

" 'Well, send them in.'

"I never bothered, and didn't expect to hear from them again. But they were desperate in those days and in due course I signed up for a program leading to a diploma in education and began to receive the princely sum of eight pounds a week.

"My years of education at university and training college remain almost a total blank. I remember learning that the word *education* comes from the Latin *educare*, to lead out, but little else. Nor at that time did I think that anything was of much value. However, I did enjoy 'prac teaching,' as we called it, and spent some time at various city and country schools."

Although he was trained as a math and science teacher, James was given a grade nine English class in his second year of teaching, and as he describes it, he brought to this classroom "a competence in the language and a liking, but not a love, for literature." He felt that he could write in sentences, he liked Dickens and Shakespeare, and expected the same of his students. "I don't think I taught them anything," he muses. "I just expected it to rub off. I don't think I've entirely lost that attitude."

Drifting again, he resigned from the Education Department of Western Australia and set out for England, where he planned to work and teach for a couple of years. He received a place in a master's program at the University of Leicester, and after completing a master's degree in English, took a teaching position at a little grammar school in Berkshire. He was given the books to teach and told to prepare the boys for their A levels at the end of the year. He taught by talking about the books with the class. As James explains, "I did most of the talking, although I think I employed the Socratic method, not for any pedagogical reason, but because it was boring listening to myself all the time. It was common sense to teach that way. I began to enjoy teaching because I was learning so much myself. . . . I didn't really begin to understand or appreciate literature until I had to teach it. Today I look back at those two years at a traditional academic grammar school as part of my own education."

It was only after those two years of on-the-job training that James felt "in any way competent to teach." When he came to Canada after the years in England, he again returned to university and completed a B.Ed., but as before, he found the education courses of little or no value. What helped him much more, he felt, were the academic courses he was allowed to take as part of his B.Ed. program, courses such as the ones he took in mythology and Literature in Religion.

He deplores the fact that the emphasis in schools today is so much on process and on group work, and worries about the level of the content that is being processed. He wants, as he says, for students to "come out of school knowing some things—not just knowing how to do things." That is one reason why he fills even his digressions with content-rich anecdotes, with information that is part of the cultural heritage and that should be part of the students' storehouse of knowledge to process. He almost winces when he recalls his own son's school experience and the "easy ride" he had in high school. "I am really upset," he says, "when students describe school as a joke and boast about how little they have to do." This is not how he wants students to assess his classes and his teaching. He does not want to be an "easy credit."

A few years ago James was granted a sabbatical by his school division and, together with his family, he spent a year in France, in order to study the language, to pursue the connections between French and English and the ways in which word meanings changed as they became part of the English language. This year had a strong impact on James' own teaching stance. In Europe, he saw again what seemed to him to be a much more serious attitude to education, and it reinforced for him the legitimacy of his own views on schooling. He turns the conversation back to his experience in the British school system, and it too stands in sharp contrast to North American schooling practices. James is concerned that students are not being challenged, that subjects are being glossed over and handled in a superficial manner. He feels that students seldom experience the satisfaction of achievement after having worked hard at something. He sees how excited some of the accelerated students are after finishing a project or a course that they have worked hard on. He sees that the demanding oral exam at the end of their course work is a "climax to their year, and therefore the year doesn't end in a whimper." He sees the exhilaration of these students after the exam and the sense of accomplishment that they feel, and is concerned that the rest of the student body is not equally challenged, and therefore never experiences that same sense of accomplishment and exhilaration. "I am convinced," he says, "that students respond according to the demands placed on them, and for the most part, we don't ask enough of them. . . . We don't teach in depth. The intellectual exercise is missing. The juices don't flow."

James' concern about the quality of education extends beyond the classroom to the training that teachers receive at schools of education. He does not place much value on teacher education programs, but he does value being knowledgeable in the subject area that one teaches. "There was a time when people in education were educated," he laments. Now, however, there does not seem to be that same emphasis on subject area knowledge, and students become teachers knowing less about the subjects they teach. They have "less education and more training," and based on his own experience, James feels that "you don't learn much in the training programs."

James has been at his present school for 10 years, and he wonders whether that isn't long enough. He would like to teach at an international school in England, and from there he could easily make trips to France. His wife would like that too, because, as he explains, "her heart's in Europe as well." In the meantime, though, as long as he is still here, he is rewarded by those students who want to learn. He is encouraged by "those students who care, those students who show interest." So he tailors his literature selections and the course content toward those novels or plays that students express interest in and that he feels have literary merit. But he senses that that is not enough. He thinks he had better become more familiar with the popular culture his students are immersed in. If he is going to work with television in order to counter some of its influence on his students, he will have to watch television and become familiar with classroom approaches to media literacy. He recognizes that partly as a result of the new curriculum, students are resisting his frontal teaching style: "My teacher-centered approach isn't working as well as it used to. Students are conditioned to a different approach, to doing things themselves. But I refuse to teach Shakespeare that way, to put them in groups to do their own reading. Attention has to be paid to the language—to the poetry of the language."

On several occasions James has offered his view on group work, which is a core concept within the new curriculum. He shows me a tenth-grade paper that is poorly done. He has given the student a mark of four out of ten and explains to me that this particular student wanted to transfer out of the class because he felt he was being marked unfairly. James felt that his work was representative of students who had done a lot of group and oral work and had been marked as part of a group. He concludes with the statement that "on individual, written assignments, his performance is very poor. This is what we're turning out." James uses groups and group projects for oral work only. He is very committed to dramatizations of scenes from literature and considers the drama assignments he gives students among the most meaningful and most important of assignments. His tenth-grade class is rehearsing scenes from *Great Expectations*, in which each character is played by two students, one portraying the character's public persona and one representing his private persona or alter ego. The two students who represent one character stand behind each other and move together through the scene, the private persona behind the public character. As the lines of the character in the novel are delivered, the private persona adds the thoughts, comments, and feelings that, although not articulated in the actual scene being dramatized, are very much in keeping with the personality and motivation of the public character. This type of dramatization exercise serves several purposes for James. He feels that the students get closer to the language of the literature in this way. It becomes their own as they learn it and use it to project thoughts, feelings, and emotions to their listening audience. Dramatizations of this nature also require students to move from just reading to a level of interpretation, necessary in order to script the part for the private persona. Students choose their own groups for these dramatizations. James feels that students work better if they are working with people they have chosen to work with. He acknowledges that the new curricular way of thinking requires heterogeneous groupings, but he does not subscribe to the concept, because so often the brightest ones end up doing all the work and the weaker students or the unmotivated ones contribute little or nothing. "Not all kids learn well in groups," he says. When I suggest that one of the reasons behind the thrust for heterogeneous groupings in collaborative learning settings is the development of self and heightened self-esteem, James sighs and says, "I'm not sure that's what we should be concentrating on. That happens all the time. Thirteen years is a long time in school. Students talk to each other and build social relationships the whole time—after classes, between classes, and on weekends. So we should devote school time to schooling." But he believes that "the climate is against academic schooling." James recognizes that he is out of step with the march of surrounding things, but nevertheless he continues to reject what he perceives as the emphasis in · the new curriculum "where English becomes a springboard for other things, . . . where teachers make students feel good." He doesn't want to be considered a facilitator—"a dreadful word." Instead, he describes himself as "a traditional teacher, a talker, digresser, questioner. One who devotes school time to schooling."

There has been some pressure for teachers to adopt the methods in the new curriculum, but for the most part, James says, "We can still do our own thing in the classroom." He knows that there are a number of teachers who only pay lip service to the new curriculum because it is politically wise to do so, but don't implement it in their classrooms. At first James ignored the curriculum, but finally he decided to speak out against it, and now he says, "I feel good about going on the record against it, because I believe in freedom of expression and the importance of free discussion, and especially the freedom to use those teaching methods which work for a particular teacher."

As an English teacher he wants to instill a love of literature and a love of language in his students. "Love of language is important. If students can feel the beauty of the language without even knowing why, that's important. Literature," he continues, "is more important than anything because it's the repository of everything that's gone before. It's the link between present, past, and future. It's the most important because it's the subject that offers the most opportunity for influencing other things—moral and personality development. Through literature kids become more tolerant and open-minded. I really think literature does make for open-mindedness. Kids should be encouraged to keep reading so they can find out about themselves and the world. They may not be mature enough to appreciate it now, but they should keep reading. They'll find themselves later on."

James wants to instill a love of learning and an intellectual curiosity in his students and then provide challenges that will allow his students to feel the "satisfaction that comes from work well done." He would like students to respond to literature and find their own answers in it. "Ideally," he says, "the curriculum should be based entirely on literature, reading it and responding to it in all kinds of ways—orally and in writing—responding to the ideas in literature, the language in literature, and the people in literature in order to learn about ourselves." James rejects the dictates of the new curriculum to separate the course into a study of the literary and the transactional use of language, that is, language employed to get things done. If literature were studied as he envisions it, with proper attention paid to the language, he maintains that "language survival would look after itself."

James has definite ideas about the purpose and the goals of English, but he worries that he might not be achieving these goals. Although he is convinced that English is the most interesting subject to teach because it is so broad, it is also "the least tangible of the subjects to teach and to measure." James hopes that what he teaches leads students to an appreciation of literature or to a greater understanding of self, but he does not know. He chooses the books he teaches not on the basis of a well-thought-out plan established at the beginning of the school year, but rather, as he explains it, he follows his whims. He teaches some books because he thinks students will enjoy them, and others because students have voted for them in class. He teaches some things, like *Paradise Lost*, because he enjoys them so much himself. At times his choice is determined by what is available in the book room, and at other times it is directed by events outside the classroom. When *Romeo and Juliet* appeared on the city ballet's fall program and special performances were announced for school groups, James immediately changed his plans to start *A Man for All Seasons* and read through *Romeo and Juliet* with his class before he took them to see the ballet performance. He has not been able to do what the research literature in education has, over the last few decades, exhorted teachers to do—reduce his large goals to precise activities that will lead logically and incrementally to the measurable achievement of that larger vision. "I don't have specific objectives," he worries. "It's piecemeal, fragmented. Where's the sequence? That's what worries me. What have they learned? In history and math, if the teacher can present the content well, the kids will learn, and there's a much more concrete knowing at the end of the year as to what has and what hasn't been learned. In math you can set out to teach certain laws and then test for them at the end. But you don't have that kind of clarity in English."

The problem, however, doesn't lie entirely with the nature of the subject matter. James assumes some of the responsibility, too. He speculates that over the years, a decline in his own energy level might be the reason why his teacher-centered approach is no longer as effective as it once was. Or possibly the reason lies in the fact that students now are so much more conditioned to a different teaching approach, having come through a system where more and more frequently the emphasis is on a student-centered, group process methodology. But then he rallies and concedes that the pessimistic turn in his conversation is temporary. "In June you feel tired, depressed. You wonder what you've accomplished. But in September there's a rebirth of enthusiasm and eagerness. I still haven't lost my idealism," he concludes.

In James' view, a good teacher is someone "who has something to say, who can inspire students and invoke a love of the subject. A good teacher is one who can express things clearly and is patient enough to work with individuals. Most important, it is someone who finds satisfaction in teaching kids." He readily acknowledges that as a teacher he plays a central role in the classroom, and that he is a "talker, a digresser, a questioner." It is important to him that students leave his classes, as he says, "knowing some things—not just knowing how to do things." Consequently, even when he digresses, these digressions are, as he puts it, "content-laden." At times he begins his classes with a discussion of political issues: "Let's take a minute to talk about the latest political crisis: the Armenians in Azerbaijan." After a few minutes devoted to current affairs, he encourages the class to watch the news on television, and then returns to the literature being studied. At other times he tries to relate the current affairs discussion to the literature being studied: "Let's talk about events in Eastern Europe to see if there's any similarity to the situation in Rome at the time of Julius Caesar." And when the class reaches Act IV, scene i in *Julius Caesar,* James says, "Let me tell you what they're doing. They're doing what's happening in Romania. They're deciding who will live and who must die. They've got a long list and they're going down it. It's a purge."

Throughout the reading of the play, James stops to focus on images, allusions, and unusual language usage. He tells students that, "Shakespeare can't resist inserting pictures that explain what he means," and directs them to look for the images. When his tenth-grade class reading *Julius Caesar* reaches the reference to the Colossus of Rhodes, James interrupts the reading to focus on allusions. He asks the class, "If after a great season our school's football team is defeated by team X and we say they met their Waterloo, what do we mean?" Several students explain, and James continues: "Why do we say that?" One student replies, because Napoleon was defeated at Waterloo, and explains as much as he remembers of the historical event. James elaborates on this explanation and then tells the class that this is an example of a historical allusion. A student asks, "What about 'Caesarian'?" James says, "Yes," helps the student to explain the term, and then uses the phrase "Herculean strength" as a further illustration. He concludes with an explanation of the origin of the phrase "turn a blind eye," and then, having prepared the ground, finally he asks the class: "Now what does the Colossus of Rhodes mean as an allusion?"

Recognizing images and understanding allusions adds to the richness of the reading experience, and in one of his essays, entitled "A Body of Knowledge," James elaborates on the importance of knowing things:

> One of the pleasures of reading is recognition of the familiar. It may be the recognition in a fictional character of a trait which the reader has witnessed in the real world, or it may be the recognition of a subtle reference to a person or event or idea from the literary background which the writer hopes the reader shares. This allusiveness of literature offers additional emotional and intellectual satisfaction, and such pleasure comes from a knowledge, however acquired, of our literary and cultural past. To sacrifice this knowledge at the altar of process in our English curriculum is to deny to the student reader some of the pleasure of shared experience with the author.
>
> Even the most popular forms of entertainment often presume some elementary knowledge of literature in the audience. We have all experienced the surprise and delight of the student who noticed and understood a literary allusion in the previous evening's television fare.
>
> More important, of course, is the fuller understanding and enjoyment of literature which comes from a knowledge of earlier works. How dull to stumble through a text strewn with incomprehensible allusions! How much more meaningful is "The Parable of the Old Man and the Young" to the boy who remembers his Bible stories, or "Ulysses" to the girl who devoured her Greek myths, or *Brave New World* to the student well acquainted with Shakespeare!
>
> Surely, our students should be familiar with some of the characters and stories on which our literature is founded. Northrop Frye considers the Biblical and classical archetypes as important in the teaching of English as the times table in mathematics. Without them, further growth is limited. To these add Shakespeare who has become central to our language and culture. It is not enough merely to know *how* to read, write, speak, listen, and think; if a student is

to grow, he must know something *about* Abraham and Odysseus and Romeo and Juliet.

Knowledge builds on knowledge. The flash of recognition is the proof of learning, the sense of accomplishment, the incentive to continue. Of course we should not teach literature simply for its content as was once the practice. Nor should we regard the teaching of literature simply as a means to an end. What happens in the text is important, and the characters that we meet are, in a sense, real and worthy of being remembered. They will stride through the pages of later books in a different guise, and may be conjured up by an author at any time.

Teachers' essays have not generally counted as part of the formal knowledge base about teaching because they are personal and often based on the seemingly narrow perspective of a single teacher. But it is precisely these characteristics that recommend them. The topics that teachers choose to write about reveal what matters to them, and thus they provide a truly emic perspective. It is evident from James' writing that it is important to him that students acquire a knowledge of their literary and cultural past, for without this, "further growth is limited." It is the role of the teacher to lead students to this knowledge. This concept of leading is a recurring thread in the weave of James' story. As Holland (1968, 1975) suggests, readers respond to a text by projecting onto it and by taking from it that which is compatible with the reader's identity theme. As each event of the text does or does not act out the reader's characteristic expectancy, compatible with the identity theme, the reader does or does not establish a positive relation toward it. The only element James remembered and abstracted from the text of his teacher education was that the word *education* comes from the Latin *educare*, to lead out. And this quality of leading students to knowledge has characterized James' teaching practice throughout his career. He writes that "a teacher can only find meaning in what he is doing by teaching, by making a difference to someone's life." His way of making that difference is not to impose a specific agenda on students, but rather to prepare for students the opportunities to learn, and then to lead them toward those opportunities. Dewey (1916), in writing about the relationship between students and teachers in a learning situation, maintains that the teacher can only provide the conditions that stimulate thinking and learning. When the teacher has "taken a sympathetic attitude toward the activities of the learner by entering into a common or conjoint experience, all has been done which a second party can do to instigate learning. The rest lies with the one directly concerned"

(p. 160). In tracing the development of his own teaching style, James says of his first years in the classroom, "I don't think I taught them anything. I just expected it to rub off. I don't think I've entirely lost that attitude." In his mind the transfer of knowledge from expert knower to student is neither guaranteed nor direct, although it is hoped that something will "rub off," something will make a difference. And, as if to echo Dewey, he adds, "As much depends on the class as the teacher."

Although his teaching style is the same for each group, the responses he receives differ dramatically. James' tenth-grade class can be described as a group of eager and enthusiastic learners, and his gifted class as very attentive and responsive, but the same cannot be said of his twelfth-grade class. The tenth graders walking into class can be overheard asking each other, "How many plays did Shakespeare write? Thirty-seven or thirty-eight?" They are more involved, more responsive during current affairs discussions, than is the grade twelve class. As a group, the tenth graders seem eager to please as they script and practice their drama presentations for *Great Expectations*. They are more intent on doing their work, and on occasion six or seven students at a time vie for the opportunity to answer questions in class. The enriched class, too, demonstrates its attentiveness through conscientious note-taking and ready answers to James' questions. In his twelfth-grade class, however, there are a number of students who would rather talk, complete other homework, stare into space, or sleep than participate in the ongoing English class. Of these students James says, "There are so many students who don't care, so if there's even one who wants to do a particular play, I would do it for that one person." On another occasion he says, "When you look around you may see them restless, but one or two are focusing on the poetry of the language and I do it for them." Or, in reference to a novel he says, "A number of students won't like it but there are always some who really do, and for those half-dozen kids I would teach it." He realizes that for the most part he teaches to a few students only, to those who care, those who want to learn. He acknowledges that he does not spend enough time with those who have a negative attitude or those who do not want to be helped. Yet in many ways the extra time he gives these students to complete their reading, the patience he shows in dealing with their incomplete assignments, and the many makeup opportunities he allows them for work not done—all of these act as invitations for students to join in the experience of learning.

On one occasion, as James prepares to hand out a test on a novel that the class has just finished studying, Moira asks if she can spend the time reading rather than writing the test, since she has not completed the novel yet. James agrees and indicates that the retest will be one week later, on March 22. On March 23, having marked the previous day's retest, James tells the class that those who did not do well on the retest because they still had not finished reading the novel would be given yet another week to complete their reading.

During a class reading of *Romeo and Juliet* several students yawn, and a few seem to be sleeping with their heads on their desks. James notices one of them and says, "Nancy, are you with us?" She lifts her head from the desk and he continues, "This is a magical scene," as if he were inviting her to share in the magic. Brad, another student who is seldom on task, who rarely has his work done, and who is usually disturbing the students around him, is patiently tolerated because, James explains, "He isn't mean, sullen, or underhanded." When Brad comes in to discuss with James a makeup opportunity for the test he has just failed, James offers him several options and then gives him yet another extension on the due date for a book he was to have read. In these ways James provides opportunities for students to learn. He is neither forceful nor insistent in his approach, but invites and leads his students to a world of literature that he knows can be very meaningful to their lives.

James is clearly a shy, introverted person. And as someone who values his privacy, he is understandably not as forthcoming in his auto-biographical stories. In response to a request to recall any biographical data that might have some bearing on his professional practice, James replied that he is "reluctant to dredge it up if it's not there immediately." Consequently, our conversations centered more on present beliefs than on past experiences. He does, however, speak of his "rather unhappy time at school" when there was no one who noticed, cared for, or took an interest in him. And he recalls twice being unfairly punished by the headmaster. Clearly this remembrance is painful. It has remained with him and has influenced his teaching. The influence is evident in the patience he displays with students like Moira, Brad, and Nancy. It is also evident in the sensitivity he shows toward students, in the interest he takes in them, and in the extra time he spends with them after school. For a period of time during one point in the school year, he meets with a group of students at 5:00 P.M. because they have asked for extra time to review Milton. Another group meets with him after school and on Saturday mornings for drama rehearsals. Four students from James' enriched class scripted a dramatic presentation of the scene from *Crime and Punishment* where Raskolnikov is about to confess to Sonya. They did it so well that James encouraged them to enter a divisional drama competition, and now they are in rehearsal. For the class presentation, the group had scripted and practiced the scene on their own, with only minimal assistance from James, but now for the competition he says he isn't sure whether he should "step in at this point and make suggestions here or there or just let them do it as their own thing." He decides in favor of the latter, offering support by his presence and making only occasional suggestions. James comments: "I spend a lot of time helping students after regular hours. It doesn't hurt my standing with the principal, who wants her staff to care about kids, but I don't do it for any altruistic reason. It is personally satisfying."

Just as he would have wanted to be noticed and encouraged to take a more active part in school activities, James notices the individuals in his class who merit special consideration or attention. He becomes aware of one student who is encountering problems with his immigrant status and makes inquiries on his behalf. Kimberly, another student, also receives individual attention from James. He says of the writing in her journal, "She has the most succinct style I've seen in a long time." In the written dialogue that he carries on with Kimberly in her journal, James quotes poetry back to her, encourages her with comments such as, "Perhaps you have the germ of a story here," and suggests that she consider entering writing competitions. James' attention is also drawn to Susan, whom he describes as "sensitive, polite, serene, a model type of student." She, too, wrote poetry in her journal, "fragmented free verse that held a lot of anger and bitterness." He talked to her because he was concerned that Susan personally might be feeling the anger and hostility that the persona in her poetry conveyed, but she didn't want to discuss the subject. James, honoring her privacy, as he would want his to be honored, didn't pursue the matter any further. But by making the gesture, he has shown Susan that someone has noticed, someone cares.

Barnes (1976) describes the traditional transmission teacher as one who:

1. Believes knowledge to exist in the form of public disciplines which include content and criteria of performance,
2. Values the learner's performances insofar as they conform to the criteria of the discipline,
3. Perceives the teacher's task to be the evaluation and correction of the learner's performance, according to criteria of which he is the guardian, and
4. Perceives the learner as an uninformed acolyte for whom access to knowledge will be difficult since he must qualify himself through tests of appropriate performance. (pp. 144–145)

James describes his teaching style as traditional and teacher-centered. "I'm not a faciltator—a dreadful word. Not a teacher who tries to get kids to get things out of themselves. I try to get them out myself, for better or worse." He wants students to leave his classes knowing something, and evaluation of their knowledge plays an important part in his teaching practice. The chalkboard in his classroom generally carries a list of the due dates for essays, presentations, recitations, tests, and makeup opportunities—a mix of oral and written evaluation methods. Although he recognizes that some students have a great deal of difficulty with exams, he feels that at least those students wanting to go on to university should be required to take them. Teachers should give more thought to the value of oral examinations. He feels that by speaking with students about *Macbeth* for half an hour, he can "get a very clear understanding of their knowledge of the play" and can therefore evaluate more precisely. As a further endorsement of exams, and especially challenging oral exams, he refers to the enriched class and the sense of satisfaction and accomplishment that those students feel after coming out of their required oral exams. "There have to be some standards," he concludes, and one way of establishing and maintaining these is through exams.

In terms of his views on knowledge and evaluation, James exemplifies what Barnes (1976) describes as a transmission teacher. But what Barnes' definition fails to convey is that the personal, human qualities that a teacher brings to the implementation of a transmission or any other model of teaching breathe into that model a life that makes it not nearly as cold and mechanical as the textbook definition implies. On the question of evaluation, for instance, although James' views do not fit into current patterns of thinking, the application of his views shows him to be much more person- than discipline-centered. He admits that if Brad's marks at the end of the year are close to a pass, he will certainly be passed because his attitude has been improving and he is starting to make an effort. And of Betta, who still has not decided on the topic of her major literary project one week before it is due, he says, "I don't want to fail her." He describes her as honest, good, and capable. He knows she has ability. She was part of the student-directed and -produced presentation of *A Midsummer Night's Dream*, which proved to be "fantastic despite everyone's misgivings because it was entirely student run." Although it is not directly related to the work required for her literary project, James would take this kind of involvement into consideration when making evaluation decisions. James imbues his style of transmission teaching with humanness and caring. Although he sees himself as knowing, in the transfer of this knowledge James does not, as Barnes (1976) suggests, "perceive the learner as an uninformed acolyte" (p. 145). Through his questions, James draws on his students' knowledge. He values their contributions, and the invitational quality of his language encourages student creativity and response. At one point during the reading of *Julius Caesar*, James says to the class, "Now we're coming to the scene we've been waiting for. We need a great crowd of people." Some students volunteer to read a part, and others are given a part to read. Then James continues, "Imagine the scene," and he sets it for the class, establishing a contrast between this and the previous scene. He asks the students to imagine a director directing the movements of the crowd and asks them to "Imagine what's happening between the lines." On other occasions he asks students, "How would you do this scene if you were a director?" With reference to the line, "Alas thou hast misconstrued everything" (V, iii, 84), James asks, "Would anyone like to argue that that statement applies more to Brutus?", and several students respond with their opinions and explanations.

During a discussion of *Catcher in the Rye* with his twelfth-grade class, James asks, "Do you see any similarity between Holden and Hamlet? Now there's a good exam or essay question."

"Yeah, better write it down," a student mutters good-naturedly.

"They're both introspective," James continues. "Do you know anyone like Holden? It's the question we always need to ask in literature. Is this character true to life?"

After some discussion of this, they move on to the fact that *Catcher in the Rye* is a frequently censored novel, and James asks students their opinion: "Do you find the book immoral or moral in its teaching?" When James announces that they will spend only one more day on the novel, one student exclaims, "We've done *Catcher* in one week? How come we spent ten months on Hamlet and whizzed through this in one week? And this is more fun."

"Are we going to do more Shakespeare?" another student asks. Although James had been intending to do poetry next, he is not given the opportunity to reply, because an animated discussion has begun on what other Shakespearean play they might read. *Romeo and Juliet* is mentioned, but some say that they studied that in ninth grade. *The Taming of the Shrew, King Lear, Twelfth Night,* and *Othello* are all suggested while James stands quietly by, listening to their talk. Finally he tells them that he is happy that they want to do more Shakespeare. Suddenly they catch themselves in their own enthusiasm and immediately deny that they want to do more Shakespeare, saying: "We just know we have to do it, so we want to have a say about what we have to do."

James smiles and says, "I'll give you a say." And he does give students their say, but reserves for himself the right to lead them beyond what they say today and what they know today. He is convinced that students will rise to meet the expectations of teachers, but feels that too often teachers don't challenge students enough. He saw the truth of this in his own son's school experience. He remarks on the contrast between North American and European schools in their practice and in their attitudes toward schooling. His experiences with European school systems, where education is taken more seriously, confirmed for him the legitimacy of his own thinking about schooling, and although he recognizes that here the "climate is against academic schooling," he for one still believes in the importance of it.

One day in class he announces that he will demonstrate a technique frequently used in French schools. He will lecture for five minutes or so as students take notes, after which he will call on them in turn to repeat back what they have heard. "It's a good exercise in listening and note-taking," he tells the class. His lecture is on the sonnet as a poetic form, and he talks about the origin, the content, and the changes over the years in the form and subject-matter of sonnets. Then the students take turns speaking his lecture back. One boy's rendition of how the Elizabethan poets took up the sonnet form is somewhat confused. James says, "Good, but you've missed some. Ben, can you correct?" The students seem eager to correct, explain, and add to each other's notes. Once the formal part of the lecture and repetition is completed, James tells students that "iambic is the natural rhythm of the English language" and encourages a few students to try making up an iambic pentameter line. He asks them what might be considered the advantages and limitations of the sonnet form and then opens his poetry book. He asks a student to read Wordsworth's sonnet "The world is too much with us" and wants the class to respond to the reading: "Any response. Anything that strikes you about the poem." The first student mentions rhyme, and the second points out that it is divided into two sections. And so the discussion continues.

James wants his students to experience the satisfaction of achievement after having worked hard at something. Consequently, in response to one student's entry in her journal that she hated analyzing and why couldn't she just read and enjoy things at face value, he replies, "You have to think about what things mean. You can't just take things at face value." Student responses to literature are important to

James: "When they [the students] connect with something in the literature, if it becomes meaningful to them, that's important. All students'
responses are appreciated because those responses are meaningful to
them, but they aren't necessarily the meaning of the literature." He
illustrates by referring to one student who had written in her journal
that the most meaningful line in *Hamlet* was, "What is this quintessence
of dust?" He was very moved when he read it, and it is a beautiful line
that he keeps thinking about now. It is also very important, he says,
because it is the line the student responded to and saw meaning in. He
adds, however, that the meaning of the line is not what she thinks it
is. She is focusing on "dust" and questioning life, and although he
acknowledges the value of this response, James says she is misinterpret-
ing. "It's a rhetorical question," he explains. "Quintessence suggests
purest form, and together with the biblical allusions of dust—all of these
make it not as negative as she interprets." Implicit in this illustration is
his belief that reading and studying literature entail more than merely
skimming the surface, and that students must move beyond initial response, must be challenged to think about what things mean.

The importance of challenging students is also evident as James
assigns a literary project to his twelfth-grade class. The students are
given several options for their project, and when James has finished
outlining these, a student asks, "Any restrictions on the books we
read?"

"Yes," James answers. "Not Stephen King. I want you to read
some things you might not otherwise read. I must approve your
choice."

Another student asks, "Could I do modern horror? Edgar Allan
Poe compared to Barker?"

"Yes, but it would be good to start with Frankenstein and Dracula
and then see how Barker borrows." After some more discussion about
what they would like to read and what will be acceptable, James concludes that "It will be a compromise between what you really want to
do and what I think will be worthwhile for you. In many cases it will be
the same."

The concept of challenge appears again in a conversation in which
he describes himself as a teacher of literature, and talks about the importance of reading and studying good literature. "If you considered yourself merely a teacher of reading, then of course it wouldn't matter what
you read—anything would do. I also believe that content is just as important as process and that it's more worthwhile to have read *Great
Expectations* than *Flowers for Algernon*, for example—not only because
Dickens is a better author, but because his works are part of the literary

canon and a student is more educated for having a knowledge of such books." He asks his classes to read one book each month as extra reading and gives a higher mark to those reading Margaret Atwood than to those reading Stephen King. The class questions the fairness of this, but his thinking is that books of literary value are more challenging and require more effort than some popular literature. A class discussion ensues, and James reports that all those students speaking in the general discussion support him, agreeing that "Stephen King was an easy read compared to literary books." When one student who has been reading Stephen King discloses, however, that she had never read before and probably would not even be reading Stephen King now if the teacher had not required it, then James sees the discussion in a different perspective and begins to step, as he says, "very carefully." He is very pleased to have her reading and certainly doesn't want to discourage her by saying that her reading is less valuable than Atwood, for instance, because in the final analysis, "having them read is what's important." In this circumstance James hovers for an instant between the clash of his strong belief in the value of literary reading and a student's compelling request to honor her ordinary reading. Philosophy is no match for a personal plea, and the momentary conflict is resolved in favor of the student.

The importance of caring for students and of respecting their feelings figures prominently in James' reminiscences of his own school days, and instances of his caring and his sensitivity to students occur with frequency in his teaching practice today. James' strong advocacy of subject matter knowledge, of traditional teaching, and of academic schooling was nurtured and reinforced by his experiences in British and French schools. The mild eccentricity he exhibits in his classroom he believes he learned from his Latin teacher. One day as we all stand outside James' classroom and wait for him to come and unlock the door, Joan gets impatient and complains "It's always the same. He's always late—then he shows up with his coffee in his hand and he has to give it to somebody to hold so he can unlock the door." There is a general murmur of agreement and another student adds, "Yeah and he never cleans up his dishes." Just then James arrives, humming a tune. He hands his coffee cup to Joan so that he can unlock the door. His desk is piled high with papers and books, and a dirty dinner plate, fork, and knife sit atop the pile. He has scheduled a test for this class but he can't find it. He searches through the books, the scraps of paper, and the news bulletins on his desk, pulls open the desk drawers, looks into the filing cabinet, scratches his head in a puzzled manner, then rummages about in his backpack and finally produces the test, a crumpled sheet of paper. But there is only one copy. The class is restless as he heads off to make copies of the test. He is back in a few minutes and they start to write. The room becomes quiet. He pulls his sweater over his head, lays it in a heap beside the dinner plate, sits down on top of an empty desk, and reads the students' journals. One by one, as the students finish writing, they hand in their tests and drift off to the washroom, the water fountain, or the lockers. Cynthia asks for her journal, which she turned in a week ago, but James can't find it. He looks everywhere. "Are you sure you gave it to me?" She assures him that she did and he turns to search again through the pile on his desk. He waves away the last test writers, and Cynthia has to go on to her next class as James keeps looking. His next class comes in but he doesn't seem to notice. Suddenly, with a sigh of relief, he pulls her journal out of one of his filing cabinet drawers. He turns to me, pointing to the red folder: "I encouraged her to read *Watership Down* because she likes James Herriot. She loved it and wrote all about it in this journal. I'd have lost her trust forever if I hadn't found it," he says as he hurries away to call her out of her class so that he can tell her that he has found the journal.

James believes that he remembers the details of his school days "because of their vivid associations" and adds, "I play the eccentric partly because if one can seem different to the kids they're more likely to remember. Crazy things stick. If you're dull and straight you won't be remembered either." Bearded, slightly dishevelled, disorganized, and absent-minded, James strides through the school with a loping gait and a coffee cup, looking at times somewhat bemused, at times deep in thought, and always slightly different.

"Not only did I drift into teaching but I drifted into whatever educational philosophy I have," James explains. Although he leafs through the occasional professional journal, he has not read anything on the teaching of literature, saying, "It's common sense, isn't it?" James frequently uses the phrase "common sense" as support or justification for decisions in his teaching practice. As Holland (1968, 1975) and Bullough (1990) would suggest, he adopts those teaching options and practices that are compatible with his identity theme, those that make sense. Clandinin (1986), recognizing that teachers already do in the classroom what makes sense to them, argues that teacher practices are coherent as a whole and resistant to changes that don't allow the whole to remain coherent. She adds that the introduction of a new program that threatens this coherence is, therefore, an extremely complex task. Bullough (1990) concurs, explaining that in the face of change, "People whose important beliefs are threatened will attempt to defend their positions, dismiss objections, ignore counterexamples" (p. 9). The philosophy of the new language arts curriculum runs counter to a number of James' important beliefs. At first he ignored the demands of the new curriculum for a student-centered classroom, but eventually he felt compelled to speak out and take a stand against it. In an essay entitled "Automatic or Standard Transmission," published in a divisional newsletter, James makes his views known:

> I was interested to read in the last issue of *Language Arts and English* that a new consultant in the Department identified "the persistence in some schools of teacher-centered and transmission-model approaches" as one of the "issues" in language arts education. Is this to be taken as implicit criticism of those schools and teachers whose strategies are not currently fashionable? If so, it seems a little hard on individuals who are sincerely practicing the teaching methods which work best for them in their classroom.
>
> I wonder why some schools are persisting in their old ways. Perhaps those teachers who are stubbornly refusing to trade in their old standard transmission model have discovered that it runs better than the new, smooth automatic with its lighter body, integrated circuitry, glossy finish, and incomprehensible instructor's manual. Anyway, what is important is that the passengers reach their destination in whichever vehicle they travel.
>
> Fortunately, the Department has acknowledged the principle of diversity in language arts instruction. In the words of the Association of English Language Arts Co-ordinators and Consultants, "The Education Department has gone on record as saying that the teaching methods and materials are negotiable in implementing this curriculum while the teaching of the objectives is not." Quite right. Different teachers have different styles and different students have different temperaments, and what works for some may not work for others. There is more than one way to reach an objective. If students are learning to read and write and speak and think and feel, *even in teacher-centered classrooms*, then let those schools be praised, not criticised! (emphasis in original)

He has, however, abstracted and inserted into his own practice those aspects of the new curriculum that make sense to him. In response to a question about what elements of his teaching have changed, he replies: "Novels. That's changed. I don't feel I have to emphasize the content as much. I'm not focusing on literary criticism only, but recognize the wisdom of seeing kids respond to literature in different ways. It's good to read more books extensively—not only some intensively."

The concept of student response is, of course, a key element in the new curriculum, and the time devoted to novel study is also an issue addressed in the document. James acknowledges that he was influenced by the new curriculum to introduce changes to his practice in these areas. He could accommodate these suggestions because they made sense, and he feels he has been able to incorporate them into his practice. Student journals have also been promoted as part of the new curriculum, and after hearing about the value of them so often, James tried them and found that "using them made sense." There is an echo of his past in the explanation that James gives for accepting journals: "Journals were a good chance to get to know introverted kids. I learned things I wouldn't otherwise have learned." As a result, he was able to help students like Brenda return to school, he was able to help Ramon sort out problems with his immigrant status, and he was able to encourage several student poets and writers. The journals made it possible for him to notice those students who might have gone unnoticed, as he once went unnoticed in school. As one journal exercise, he asks students to read Orwell's essay on his life at school. Then students write their own story, or a similar one to Orwell's, outlining their significant school experiences. The two most strongly evident characteristics of James' teaching—caring about students and emphasizing the importance of literature and subject matter knowledge—are present and captured even in this brief example from his practice. The caring element, evident in his reason for using journals, is combined with his need to lead students beyond their present and private response toward the kind of broader understanding that the reading of literature fosters.

Although honoring student responses and encouraging students to write in journals were elements of the new curriculum that fit into James' schema, he cannot accommodate the use of collaborative learning groups. One of the benefits cited for group work is that it allows students to learn through language usage. Ironically, James' criticism of groups centers precisely on the point of language. "I refuse to teach Shakespeare that way, to put them in groups and do their own reading. Attention has to be paid to the language—to the poetry of the language." There is also an element of James' own past experience that surfaces in his pronouncements about group work. "Not all kids learn well in groups," he says, and certainly it is not a style he is comfortable with. He is, as he says, an introverted and shy person in a group, who doesn't "contribute much to the conversation." It is, therefore, not surprising that he does not ask his students to learn in a small group setting. James has gone on record against both the group process as a learning method and the way in which group work has been imposed on teachers. Both the learning process and the manner of imposing it are alien to him. James is not a group conversationalist himself and, therefore, cannot advocate the process. Neither is it his wont to arbitrarily impose new learning styles on his students. He is more apt to introduce, suggest, encourage, and lead his students, and then leave it up to them if they wish to follow. He would have preferred to have encountered the concepts of the new curriculum in the same way. "It would have been better to introduce it properly, with good in-services. And if it was a good program it would have flourished. If not, it would, and it should, die." Ironically, even as teachers were encouraged to embrace transactional and process models of teaching, the professional development workshops designed to foster this very change were conducted as models of transmission teaching.

On occasion James makes an effort to have students work in groups for a portion of the class time. But his students have not been instructed in group work skills, and James does not monitor their progress. Consequently, the time spent is altogether unfruitful. The attempts are failures, only serving to reinforce James' already firmly held beliefs about learning in groups. The consistency of James' practice, the coherence and wholeness of it, are violated by the demands of the new curriculum for a student-centered, group-oriented, collaborative learning approach, and therefore he rejects them. Even when change is welcomed by teachers, it is difficult to actualize. How much more difficult when both the process and the content of a planned educational change are in conflict with the values and beliefs of the teacher. Pajares' (1992) work underscores this difficulty and the complexity of the change process. He points out that:

- Knowledge and beliefs are inextricably intertwined, but the potent affective, evaluating, and episodic nature of beliefs makes them a filter through which new phenomena are interpreted.
- The earlier a belief is incorporated into the belief structure, the more difficult it is to alter.
- Belief change during adulthood is a relatively rare phenomenon. (p. 325)

The advent of the new curriculum has, however, stimulated James to a reflective examination of his own practice. Although most of his beliefs about teaching run counter to the new curriculum, in the face of so many directives to teach differently, he is beginning to question the efficacy of his ways. "My teacher-centered approach isn't working as well as it used to," he muses. He thinks, possibly, that it could be that he has less energy now than he used to have, and certainly students are conditioned to a different approach. "If I can find something else that works, I'll do it." He is also beginning to question his thinking about content knowledge. When he was very involved with his school's Reach for the Top team, he thought that knowledge of content was very important, especially knowledge that was part of our cultural heritage. But now he is not sure, because "our Canadian culture has shifted away from its British roots. Maybe this emphasis on culture is just my culture, but it's not appropriate for everyone. Maybe we should study native myths." He doesn't know. This process of self-reflection, of questioning, and of reassessing long-held beliefs is a necessary prerequisite to new learning and to genuine change. James' movement to and fro, his acceptance of some new concepts, his slight shifts and tenuous changes in disposition—all of these represent efforts of "trying to find a place for new experiences to fit into already held beliefs" (Lester & Onore, 1990, p. 41). James' practices are based on beliefs that are solidly rooted in his past experiences and intricately bound to memories, associations, and values. Substantive changes in his practice will come about not as a result of mandating new approaches to teaching; they will occur only when he has personally worked through, accommodated, and accepted new ways of doing things, and integrated them into his beliefs.

More than two years after we had begun working together and after I was no longer a part of his classroom, James described his new practice to me, and confirmed again the gradual and personal nature of the process of change. He had just finished teaching Orwell, Huxley, and Margaret Atwood's *The Handmaid's Tale*, and in keeping with his strong beliefs of challenging students and doing more than skimming the surface of literature, he had also taught Zamyatin's *We*, which Huxley and Orwell both acknowledged as a source for their material. But at the same time that he is keeping to the old ways, James is also incorporating more and more those elements of the new curriculum consonant with his beliefs about good teaching. He has now extended his use of journals. James feels that he is moving more toward a reader response approach in his classroom, and keeping a reading response log has now become the major project for his twelfth-grade English class. He has done away with the required research paper, and instead students write a reflective essay based on their classroom and extra assigned reading. This new approach fits into James' already held beliefs. He initiated this change because in fact it is a means of achieving his goal of having students read widely. Thus the change, being consistent with his beliefs about teaching, maintains the coherence of his practice.

Reading, studying, and knowing good literature are the central components of James' teaching practice. In conversation, the special memories of teaching that he brings to the fore focus not on the teacher or the teaching method, but on literature and students' appreciation of it. In response to a question about which stories of particular students or classes have remained in his memory as examples of teaching and learning as they should be, he speaks of students who want to come to class because they enjoy English and talking about literature. He remembers enjoyable discussions and says, "Sometimes it happens once or twice per year—some years not at all, when a student says, 'Thanks, I really enjoyed that. I hadn't before.'" James reports that the accelerated students in his Milton class this year have come away wanting to read more Milton. "They've read passages to their parents, and that's very satisfying to a teacher." A small group in his Milton class asked James for extra help, and he met with them after school and on Saturday mornings. He was delighted to be asked because "here was a group of kids who wanted to learn." They were so grateful to him that they gave him a gift certificate for a book purchase. He was overwhelmed, amazed at the large sum, and also embarrassed because he enjoyed these extra classes and felt that he had already been rewarded by the students' interest in literature. Another conversation, in which James highlights the importance of literature, occurred one afternoon when James was late for our meeting. He had been detained by a former student who had just completed her first semester at an eastern university and had come to visit him. He reports that she told him how she had been influenced as a student in his class by Raskolnikov and *Crime and Punishment*. She had been thinking a lot about Raskolnikov, about freedom and breaking away. "It makes that book more worth doing," he concludes.

James acknowledges that he has always been and continues to be "a traditional teacher." His teaching practice has grown out of his personal and professional experiences and reflects his strong beliefs in academic schooling, the value of literature, and the value of "knowing some things—not just knowing how to do things." Although he realizes that his traditional teaching approach is currently unfashionable, he nevertheless continues to teach in ways that make sense to him. And he finds an ally for his teaching stance in Cusick (1973), who writes in the conclusion of *Inside High School*:

> Personally, I think the best teaching takes place when the teacher accepts his role as subject matter specialist, accepts the difference between himself and the students, and utilizes his status advantage to concentrate his efforts on instruction. That sounds simple, but I find few teachers who do it. Many confuse their instructional role with attempts to be a friend, personal

adviser, confidant, or critic of students' personal behavior. Then instead of keeping the subject before them, they spend their time watching the students to see what they want, trying to utilize the student groups to attain their own ends, or moralizing about students' personal behavior and associations which are none of their business. I think those who succeed best in public schools are those who are perhaps the most conservative in their view of their role, the most liberal in their acceptance of students. (p. 226)

Chapter 3

Raymond's Story

Raymond's eleventh-grade class has just finished reading *Macbeth*. Each day for the last several days, in small groups of four or five, scattered throughout the school—in the library, in small seminar rooms, or in the classroom—students had assumed the roles of the characters in the play and read through it act by act. Raymond had spent half of a class period introducing Shakespearean drama to his students, talking about *Macbeth* specifically and starting the class on the reading of the play. For the second half of that class the students, already in their groups, began to read on their own, and then spent the next few classes reading in groups until they had finished the play. At the beginning of each class, before the groups dispersed to their assigned reading areas, Raymond warned each group that he knew the page number, the act, and the scene that they were on, and if he noticed as he came by to visit each group that they hadn't made much progress in their reading, he would assume that they had been fooling around and they would then "have to come into the classroom to sit alone and read the play." He reminded the students that the purpose of this reading was "to get an overview of the plot." If they had questions or if they got lost or confused in the text, they were to ask each other first and turn to him for help only as a last resort. They were sent on their way to read with a final reminder to have fun while they read and to read dramatically, but also to work. As soon as the groups had settled down to read, Raymond began to circulate among them and to ask quick questions to check comprehension: "What happened yesterday? Who killed Duncan? What part did Lady Macbeth play?"

Several of the groups seemed totally absorbed in their task, gave fine dramatic readings, and sailed through the play. Other groups stopped frequently to question each other and sort out points of confusion in the plot development. Raymond moved briskly from one group to the next, asking quick questions and waiting only for brief responses before moving on to the next group. When a student greeted Raymond's arrival to his group with the questions, "Is Banquo dead? Did he murder?" Raymond's response was, "I'm not telling you." In checking another student's understanding of the text, Raymond asked the boy to explain the meaning of a particular line. The student tried to paraphrase, hesitated, tried again, but couldn't seem to frame the essence of the line. Raymond asked him if he had a sense of the meaning of the line, and when the student assured him that he did, Raymond directed him to "keep going" and moved immediately to the next group. Ten minutes before the end of the class, all the students returned to the classroom in order to record in their journals what had happened in the plot during their reading that day.

After three classes given over to reading time, everyone has reached the end of Act V, and now each group must present a plot outline to the whole class and illustrate it on the overhead projector. After the first group has presented its outline, Raymond calls for questions from the class and tells them that "even if something is so unclear that you don't know how to ask, try anyway. Remember, this part of the class is strictly there to make some sense of the plot."

Trevor asks Raymond why McDuff's family is killed. Raymond responds with "Good question," and turns it over to the group that is presenting for an answer. The group isn't sure, and so Raymond suggests that they all check Act IV.

"Who's got the page?" he asks.

"Fifty-four," says one of the group members.

"Okay," Raymond begins, "let's look. 'For none of woman born/ Shall harm Macbeth.' How does that tie in with Trevor's question of why they kill McDuff's family?"

A student suggests that the motive might have been "to revenge," upon which Raymond corrects him and says "it's avenge," and goes on to ask further questions:

"Who kills McDuff's family? Any other possibilities for killing McDuff's kids?" The students have some difficulty answering Raymond's questions, and he directs them to turn to page six: "What did the witches say? You're yawning, Jeff. Get with it."

Raymond is a wiry, energetic, and athletic man. He moves, acts, and speaks quickly, fairly flying from one question to the next. He wants his class discussions to "snap like popcorn" and doesn't tolerate inattentiveness or sleepyheads in his classroom. Jeff knows this and stifles his yawn. He tries to look alert and asks a question: "Would his son have more power?" But Raymond, in keeping with his beliefs about the importance of students finding their own answers, replies, "I don't know. I just have an opinion like you."

The questions continue for a while and then the next group comes forward to present its plot outline to the class. Again there are questions directed at the group or at Raymond. One student asks, "Who killed Lady Macbeth and why?"

Becky replies, "She killed herself, didn't she? She went crazy." Then she reads from the text to support her statement. Rob disagrees and offers his theory that Lady Macbeth was killed by a mob. Raymond summarizes: "There are two positions. Becky says it's suicide and Rob says she was killed by a mob. We'll have to examine this suspicion."

When all the plot outlines have been presented, Raymond re-arranges the groups to form units of four, and explains that their task now is to count up the soliloquies that precede and occur during or after each murder. The purpose of this, he tells the students, is to have them "see the pattern of Macbeth as a thinking man and a man of action." The students are used to working together, and so they shift into their new groupings quickly as Raymond tells them, "You've got seven minutes." Immediately he begins to circulate among the groups, making comments and fielding questions. To one group he says, "You should be paging through the book," while to another he comments, "Good, excellent, terrific! Move quickly. We only have a few more minutes."

One student asks, "Do they say much in the play before the murder of Banquo?"

"That's what you have to establish," Raymond answers. "If you don't think there's much, then say so and we'll see what the other groups say."

"Has he killed him here yet?" Sean asks, pointing to a line in the play. Raymond looks over his shoulder, reads the line—"If it were done, when tis done, then 'twere well/It were done quickly"—looks expectantly back at Sean, and waits until another student in Sean's group suggests an answer to the question.

Raymond moves to where I am sitting at the side of the room and explains that he feels comfortable getting to know a book by paging through it, and wants the students to experience that too. Then, pre-cisely seven minutes into the group work, Raymond calls the discus-sions to a halt and the whole class forms one circle, which Raymond pulls in as tightly as possible. They begin to look at the soliloquies to see how many words Macbeth speaks, to find in the soliloquies the pattern of Macbeth as both a thinking man and a man of action. They read Macbeth's words before, during, and after Duncan's murder, and a student asks, "What about after Macbeth kills Duncan—when he kind of seems to be asking for forgiveness?"

Another student replies, "But he's speaking to Lady Macbeth."

A third student suggests, "He could just be saying it—and it's really to himself but she's just there." To this Raymond replies, "Hadn't thought about it. Shrewd observation. We want to examine that possibility." After some more discussion of the soliloquies surrounding this first murder, the class moves on to the soliloquies related to Banquo's murder. Raymond notices Wendy's inattentiveness and calls to her, saying, "C'mon, Wendy, you're dreaming. I want everyone working in their books when we're doing this." They continue with Macbeth's speech about MacDuff, at the end of Act IV, scene ii, and Raymond asks, "Any difference between what he says here and when he says, 'Is this a dagger which I see before me?' Is this about ideas or feelings? Is he talking about feelings or ideas? Quick, before you fall asleep here. Let's do the mass murders. This is boring, you guys, but it'll save you hours of work. Look at these soliloquies. What do you notice?"

One student responds, "In the beginning he seems to think. At the end he just acts."

Raymond asks if there is any disagreement with this assessment. The class says, "No," and he suggests that they "leave it as a possibility." The last few minutes of the class are to be spent writing, and Raymond gives the students their writing assignment: "Your friend asks you to betray another friend, or the parents you love, or a teacher you respect. Decide who [sic] you will betray and how you will do it. Then in a paragraph write the thoughts that go through your mind as you think about whether you should or not, and how you'll do it. Write. Let your minds go. I'll write with you."

One students asks if Raymond will read what they are about to write. Raymond replies, "We'll use it in our groups tomorrow," and sits down at his desk to write. Six minutes later he holds up the page that he has written and directs the students to finish theirs at home. The class is over, and as the students prepare to leave, Raymond tells them that they have now had four classes on Macbeth, that they will have another week, and that they will have to memorize twenty lines, either consecutive lines or phrases of their choosing that make up twenty lines.

"It's a delight to know lines from Shakespeare," he tells his class. "You can insult people."

"Is that like when people say, 'Et tu, Brute'?" one student asks.

Raymond smiles and nods. "Desks in straight lines," he reminds the class before they leave. "Thanks. See you tomorrow."

Raymond is an excellent host to those visiting in his classroom. He shares his thoughts, explains his actions, and invites comments and feedback from those who have come to watch him teach. As always, once the class has left, and after he has talked to any students who have remained behind, Raymond turns to me to talk about the *Macbeth* class I've just observed.

"This is a weak group," he says of the class. "I'm a period behind from when I did it with another eleventh-grade class seven years ago. I've changed the format, but still—they're weak." Then we begin to speak of just how his teaching style or format has changed. There was a time when he held center stage in the classroom; he performed as a teacher and became a popular star with his students. He recalls how he was surrounded by girls at school dances, girls who all wanted to dance with him because they admired him. He had a high profile in the class-room and became, as he explains it, "a legend in the school." He felt that he could be a good teacher only if he "imposed [himself] on the learning." But, he says, "there's an uneasiness in people that keeps them moving—either to different books or to different schools. It's an uneasiness almost akin to the artist's." In his own case, he explains, it led him to move from one teaching style to another. When he started teaching he had taken only three courses in English and, therefore, had only a tenuous grasp of his subject area. After taking courses every summer for a number of years and devoting his sabbatical year to taking a pre-master's degree in English, he felt more confident as a teacher of English. However, he continued to teach in a teacher-centered fashion, to talk to and act for his "captive audience of students" in order to win their admiration. In 1983, ten years after the completion of his pre-master's course work, Raymond took part in some classroom re-search that sought to compare the effectiveness of traditional teacher-centered approaches to studying poetry with the effectiveness of a reader-response-based, collaborative learning approach. In an essay entitled "Teaching Students to Read Poetry Independently," Raymond documents his involvement in this project. He describes his teaching as having been based on "a carefully structured, teacher-centered model" and continues:

> I was able to control and dominate the learning. My role in this experiment was a radical departure from the way in which I had taught before. I had to break with a whole series of conditioned responses. Needless to say, I was in pain. I had to surrender much of the control I had exercised over students.

But the evidence from this experiment pointed to the effectiveness of a response-based, collaborative learning approach, and so as a result of his involvement in this project, Raymond began to question his teacher-centered approach and to consider changes in his teaching style. Eventually he began to implement the kind of student-centered collaborative model that he had witnessed in the research project. He encouraged his students to become independent readers, to search for their own answers in literature, and to recognize that many answers are possible and indeed acceptable. Although the research experiment that he had been a part of convinced Raymond of the validity of such a teaching approach, he reports that he became quite depressed when he finally implemented the model in his own classroom. As he subdued his usual antic classroom disposition and made way for the students to become the focal point in his class, as he stepped aside and encouraged them to come forward, he became less visible and his popularity waned. For the first time that year at graduation the girls didn't flock around him and clamor to dance with him. In fact, they ignored him. He recognized in retrospect that he was psychologically not ready to give up his popularity, to give up the center-stage role in the classroom, and what he referred to as "the adulation of the students."

Nevertheless, he continued along his new path and molded the student-centered collaborative learning approach that he had first been a part of in the experimental study into a model uniquely his own. The original study was rooted in a sociopsycholinguistic approach to reading, and based largely on Rosenblatt's transactional theory of reader response. Raymond refers to his own teaching approach as "response teaching," but not being familiar with Rosenblatt or other reader response theorists, he defines the term in his own way. Response teaching for Raymond means that students work together in collaborative groups to become independent readers of literature, examining the assumptions inherent both in the literature and in their own lives, and "thinking on levels of engagement from which they can't extricate themselves." The teacher's role within a response model is to respond in "caring and challenging ways" to both the intellectual and emotional responses of students, to respond to the whole person. Whereas the focus in reader response theory is on the reader's transaction with the text, Raymond's definition and interpretation of response teaching places a heavy emphasis on the role of the teacher and the teacher's response to students, as opposed to an emphasis on the response to text. For Raymond, response teaching is a way of living and relating to others. "The human aspect," he says, "must be first." Response teaching for Raymond means "engaging the feelings and the mind. It means responding to the whole person—the mind, the feelings, and the body language." And he feels that this manner of responding to students must be a genuine part of the teacher's life; it must be part of a teacher not just inside, but also outside the classroom. In Raymond's view, the teacher never gives answers, "but sets up the environment so that students can catch the sparks from each other." He wants students to say what they feel and think, and he challenges them to defend their statements. "The students' responses should show the whole person. It's not just an intellectual exercise. Their responses should develop options. In a sense, I move literature into their life experience. We look at situations in literature and I ask students how they think a father would respond to this situation, or a friend. How would they decide if they had a problem? If they're facing a difficult decision, do they develop alternatives or do they go with their first response? I want to get beyond opinions to options—to a problem-solving way of life. I want students to be in an environment where they can recondition their responses. I want them to see with several eyes."

"When students respond to literature and say, 'I like this' or 'I like that,' it isn't enough," Raymond continues. "These are mere eruptions of feeling. I want to go beyond the surface. Literature isn't just for fun. There's got to be a moral streak in literature and there's got to be a way for them to see something truer today than they saw yesterday." To explain, he cites an example that he refers to frequently in our conversations. In one scene from Margaret Laurence's novel *The Diviners*, the protagonist, Morag, is introduced to her lover's wife. When students ask what would possess Dan to bring Morag home and introduce her to his wife, Raymond is able, as he explains it, to respond without fear. "If I were teacher-centered," he explains, "I would have answered their question, but answers are not important to me. Instead, I was able to say to them that they needed to examine the assumptions underlying the act. This required them to think about possibilities."

Although Raymond doesn't endorse a teacher-centered approach and doesn't see himself as teaching in a teacher-centered way, he nevertheless plays a very central role in his classroom. He chooses the materials, structures the discussion procedures, teaches and requires of the students specific behavioral, listening, and group skills, and monitors time on task very closely. He acknowledges the centrality of his role in structuring the classroom environment, but sees no contradiction in this. Rather, he feels that it is necessary, explaining that the tighter he controls the structure, the more students can explore, because, as he explains, "the structure I impose insists that students speak to each other, and thereby they learn. The group structure allows students to benefit from each other. The sparks from one might ignite another—and the paradox is that the more you become involved in the group, the more you develop as an individual. I never give a group mark, and there is never a focus on consensus, but students must cooperate and facilitate group effort, even if personality clashes exist, because as they explore different dimensions, they benefit from each other." He returns again to *The Diviners* to illustrate the importance of the structures in his new teaching style: "I taught *The Diviners* for years, thinking I had done a very good job, but invariably at the end of the novel, someone would write about Morag as a slut. But as soon as I changed from my teacher-centered approach to a cooperative teaching style, this stopped, because now female students were no longer powerless. The class was structured so that they were now in a position where they could confront males."

As another example to illustrate his teaching approach, he tells of the time he gave his students an article from *Time* magazine on Gorbachev. After they had discussed the article, he told his students that he was disappointed because they hadn't focused on certain words. He pointed these words out to them and sent them on their way with instructions to think about these words. "When they came back to class the next day, they were sharper and more attuned. Some of the response people say you shouldn't do that because you're directing the students' learning. But I don't believe that. I saw how much more aware they were afterwards."

Biblical references and allusions occur frequently in Raymond's speech, and he speaks often of his commitment and responsibility to his students. He recognizes that he has a lot of control and power, but says he wants to exert the kind of compassionate authority that Moses and Abraham had. He wants to be a caring shepherd not just for the 99, but for the 99 plus 1 in his fold. In Raymond's image of response teaching, the student is in direct contact with the text, and the teacher is like a mist surrounding both. Raymond stresses again that in a response mode the teacher's role is to challenge students and that sometimes teachers have to be cruel in doing so. "Sometimes," he says, "I have to play God with students, because I'm the referee and I have to call the shots. It's a terribly, terribly lonely moment—especially when you're called upon to humiliate them." To explain, he talks about Josh, whom he describes as a very "chauvinistic boy." One day, during a discussion in literature that revolved around male/female relationships, when Josh's opinions were becoming particularly irritating to the girls in his group, Raymond asked Josh whether he would marry his own daughter. Puzzled, Josh said no, and so Raymond suggested that he should therefore consider marrying his equal. As Raymond explains it, "This challenge buzzed in Josh's head for days, and in his group, discussion wasn't about the novel, but about these issues. That's what I'm after. I knew they had read the book," he adds, "so I didn't have to worry about that." Raymond recalls that he had to "break his stock responses" to many situations in life, and that is what he demands of the students in his classes. "I challenge them to take note of the myths they hold. That's why I've become a legend in the school," he says.

And indeed, Raymond has achieved a high profile, not only in his school, but also in the surrounding community of teachers. Teachers interested in implementing a student-centered, collaborative learning model visit and observe Raymond's classes. He welcomes these visits, eager to explain to teachers how he has taught group process skills to his students, and anxious to show visitors how group discussions in his class "snap like popcorn." He has taught students to listen carefully in group discussions, to respect each other, to build on what has already been said, and to engage ideas only when grappling with issues, without involving personalities.

On one occasion when the discussion centers on life issues, which Raymond favors, the class is called upon to decide which of two scenarios is more tragic or sad. Raymond outlines the two stories. In the first instance, a child of five runs from the house after being terrorized by her brother. She is hit by a car and killed instantly. The second scenario centers around a grown man who has been an alcoholic for years, but has rehabilitated himself and doesn't drink anymore. He visits friends one evening who insist that one drink won't matter. He tries to resist but eventually gives in, has a drink, and is hooked again. He lives a miserable six months, reflecting on his life, and then dies. In groups of four or five, students are to discuss these two cases and develop arguments for choosing one over the other as the more sad or tragic story. After fifteen minutes of loud, heated group discussion Raymond tells the class that they are now to enter their decisions in their journals and "Really argue your case, because you'll have to defend it in front of the class." They begin and the room is suddenly silent, punctuated only by an occasional burst of argument from one corner where three boys who think the second story is more tragic try to persuade one girl to their way of thinking. But she holds steadfastly to her own opinion and argues vehemently for the first story.

Small group discussions in Raymond's class are almost always followed by plenary sessions where students must argue their positions in front of the whole class. Although students are assigned the task of group leader and group recorder, the actual discussions within small groups are unstructured and spontaneous: heated if the topic is of interest, and slow if it is not, or if it centers on a novel that not everyone has finished reading. In the plenary sessions, however, Raymond insists upon structure and orderly procedures. The class forms a large circle for the plenary, and Raymond, who sits as a member of the circle, pulls it in as much as possible. One student is assigned to record the names of all those who wish to speak, and it is this student's responsibility to give others the floor in the proper order. The plenary on this day proves to be as loud and heated as the group discussions were, but in this forum Raymond does not tolerate interruptions or emotional outbursts. When the discussion threatens to become too chaotic because everyone is speaking at once, Raymond calls things to a halt, saying, "You may not interrupt. Effective debaters remember their arguments. Lawyers do that, too. Who's next?" Greg, who has been assigned to keep the speakers' order, gives a nod to one student who barely finishes her statement before the room erupts in a chorus of objections. Raymond interjects again, saying, "This is breaking down. This isn't going to work. When we interrupt others we cease to think. It's just passion." He calls again for reasoned arguments and the debate continues, punctuated from time to time by angry outbursts and vehement personal attacks. One student, visibly upset, declares that "It's stupid to argue one versus the other. Both stories are tragic. It's inhuman for us to sit here and argue." Nevertheless, the arguments continue. After twenty minutes, Raymond stops the discussion to make some observations about the group process: "What happens when people ask, 'How do you know that's more tragic? Were you there?'"

Becky replies, "You get defensive when people start lashing out at you."

"What happens to the discussion?" Raymond asks.

"It crumbles," Becky responds.

Raymond points out to the class that when discussions become emotional, they aren't effective in changing people's minds. In fact, what generally happens, he tells them, is that "people just get angrier and more firmly committed to defending their original positions, when the point of the discussion is to have them see more and more possibilities. Anyone can react emotionally, but it's important to learn to argue." He talks to them about debating techniques, about the need to supplement and qualify their statements, to give credit to previous statements, and to build on those. Then he reviews the arguments thus far, and the discussion resumes in a more measured manner.

"I still think the man's story is more tragic," Philip says. "But after listening to Dave, I can see that it was his decision and that he just made the wrong one."

As a form of closure, Raymond then asks the students to take out their journals again and write about how they feel now, having heard

so many varying viewpoints. "Can you expand now on your first response?" he asks the class. "Remember, there are a number of people
involved in each situation. To whom is it more tragic—or less? To what
degree is the other situation tragic? You can stay with your original
position, but bring the others in, too." While they write, Raymond
comments to me, "This is generally a dead group. I didn't think they
would become so passionate. Now I can build on this. Passion is necessary, but not woolliness. Teaching group skills is hard. That's probably
why some teachers don't do it—because it's a lot of work to teach and
reteach the steps of defining the task, delegating duties, and going
through the process." Seven minutes into their journal writing, Raymond calls, "Enough. Turn them in," and with nine minutes left until
the end of the class, he begins a new activity in which students role-play
a scene where one sad person is being consoled by two others.

Not only does Raymond receive many visitors who wish to observe
his teaching techniques, he has also presented his response model of
teaching at local conferences and workshops, and his classes have been
videotaped for use in a teacher education program. As an executive
member of a well-recognized national organization, Raymond has made
numerous presentations at national and international conferences on
the teaching of reading and language arts. As an impassioned spokesperson for his new way of teaching, Raymond exemplifies what he
now demands of his students: "That they restructure their conditioned
responses and consider other possibilities." Raymond speaks readily of
his before and after private and public personae. In conversation he
draws many parallels between his personal life and his teaching style
and points to the powerful influence of personal biographical events in
the shaping and changing of his professional stance.

Raymond grew up in a small, religious fundamentalist community
where the demands of farming determined his daily activities, and the
dictates of the church prescribed his thinking. An autocratic father is-
sued harsh commands to labor outside on the farm, while an equally
demanding mother monitored his faith inside the home. He attended a
rural parochial school that reinforced the teachings of his home, and
together the influences of church, school, home, and community
shaped, in Raymond's words, a man conditioned to respond in certain
ways, a man who seldom considered other options or possibilities, a
man "who needed to shake the oppressive cloak of a narrow, repressive, confining upbringing."

Although many of his schoolmates returned to the farm after high
school graduation, Raymond was not interested in farming and attended university instead. After completing a B.A., he considered going

into the ministry, but rejected that as being "too narrow." Instead, he began to give thought to law school, but received no encouragement for this decision. His father's comment was, "Another four years?" Elaine, who was later to become his wife, also discouraged him. She is, as Raymond explains it, "an idea-centered person who examined assumptions and had only contempt for law." Consequently, he set aside thoughts of law and became a teacher, a very common and acceptable professional choice for those of Raymond's community not interested in farming. There is a striking similarity in the popularly perceived functions of all three of the career possibilities Raymond considered. The roles of minister, lawyer, and teacher each call forth images of the dominating presence of a solitary figure standing in front of and speaking persuasively to a group. The common element in all three professions, the single person wielding influence over many through rhetorical skill, appealed to Raymond, and indeed it represents the way in which he taught initially. It is precisely this element, strongly developed in two of Raymond's former professors, that influenced him considerably. His high school teachers were "negative models," and Raymond vowed he would never treat students the way he had been treated. But two university professors, Jack Nielson and Daniel White, made a strong impression on him. Undergraduates sat mesmerized under the spell of Professor White's rhetorical skills, but at the same time his sharp tongue and authoritarian manner struck fear into their hearts. Raymond remembers him as a "seemingly hard, at times even cruel, yet favorite professor." Both Professor White and Dr. Nielson were known for their dramatic classroom antics and eccentric natures, and Raymond tried to emulate especially Professor White in his first years of teaching. He concludes that "teachers are frustrated actors. They need to talk, to have a captive audience. They can't find expression anywhere else." He feels that he probably didn't realize it then, but does realize now that this is the reason he became a teacher.

Besides the influence of his former professors in shaping his own teaching style, Raymond cites the influences of his family and the traumatic experiences in his own life as the two other powerful forces in his development as a teacher. His reading at university led Raymond to question the fundamentalist religious faith of his parents and the lifestyle he had been raised in, based as it was on an uncompromising patriarchal value system. Raymond had been taught to accept biblical teachings unquestioningly, to live his life by these and to consider no other possibilities. He fought fiercely against his past and feels that he has examined the assumptions underlying his old way of life, has broadened his understanding, and has systematically "restructured his conditioned responses.'' And this is what he wants his students to do when they discuss literature and think about their own lives.

But the influence of his family has also been positive in a number of ways. He credits his family with instilling a strong work ethic in him. Several of his family members are teachers or involved in church work, and are seen as being good communicators and good listeners. Raymond respects these attributes and feels that he, too, is now an able listener. His ability to listen and be sensitive came about because of what he describes as one of the most traumatic and significant experiences of his life. He describes himself before the age of thirty as having been self-righteous, aggressive, and extremely motivated. ''People probably used to find me quite offensive,'' he adds. But all that changed when at age thirty-three he began to go through ''a tremendous growing and maturing process.'' Raymond points out that Christ died at age thirty-three, a very young age, an age when he, Raymond, was just beginning to grow. He began then, as he explains, to ''rethink a whole lot of things about the way I grew up; to examine the polarities.'' He became part of a sensitivity group, in which, he says, ''I freed myself from myself. As Paul the Apostle says, you learn to eat solids.'' But just as he was gaining a solid footing on this new road of growth and self-discovery, Raymond's wife went into a deep depression that lasted five years. He describes this time as ''five years of hell'' and recalls how he could hear her screams as he walked up the sidewalk into the house after school. He knew each day that he would open the door to a house in chaos, things smashed and broken, children needing care, and a wife distraught and beside herself. So he would set about soothing Elaine, putting the house in order, cooking the meals, and then finally attending to his school work. He survived on three hours of sleep each night, but the drain on his energy as he tried to juggle school work, housework, and keeping the family together took its toll. He didn't attend church for those five years, suffered chest pains, functioned in a perpetual state of exhaustion, and eventually came to the point where he ''had nothing left.'' He sought help for himself then. A naturopath recommended a body cleansing and a new diet, and this prescription heralded a new stage in Raymond's life. His sense of physical and emotional well-being began to improve, and just then Elaine began to come out of her depression, too. ''I've been euphoric ever since she came out of her depression,'' he says. And in retrospect, he describes those hellish five years as ''a tremendous growing time; the beginning of a phoenix-like growth into beauty.'' The self-righteousness, jealousy, and aggressiveness that characterized his earlier years gave way to a compassionate, committed, loving, and understanding caring. ''And it's this,'' he says, ''that colors my relationship with students. Some people don't change as a result of traumatic experiences. I know a fellow who's been divorced three times and still hasn't changed. But for me, this traumatic experience, those five years, were a catalyst for change. They took the edge off me and made me more sensitive and a listener."

Just at this time Raymond became involved in the collaborative learning research project. He had already been reading some books on group work, and the data gathered from the research project supported a collaborative method of teaching. "It was enough," as he describes it, "to push me over the edge." It also afforded him an avenue for expressing the new sense of self that had just begun to emerge. "If I had tried this group process before, it would just have been technique. Now it works because I have a soul as well as technique. I know my weaknesses and my strengths. I've rejected polarities. I see things as a weave now, not just as black or white. I'm no longer judgmental. I have an inner peace and the kids know that there is no fear, that every question is open." Now he goes "beyond the surface" in the way that he relates to his students. He feels a genuine concern for them, and has a new understanding, especially for male/female relationships. He mentions again that as a result of his upbringing he has had to restructure all of his responses related to gender issues, but now he can say that "over the last few years, my closest allies in class have been perceptive females who have sensed my enormous compassion for personhood." His life, Raymond says, is now predicated on joy, peace, and trust, both inside and outside the classroom. He explains that the love, commitment, and trust within his marriage spills over into his classroom and lets him respond to students in genuinely caring and challenging ways. Raymond fiercely insists that there must be this harmony between public and private life, this willingness to live by the same standards inside and outside the classroom: "A good teacher must have a willingness to live by the same standards he or she expects of others, with a compassion to allow others their weaknesses without affecting his or her love for them." His classes work and his groups work, he says, because he has this integrity and he requires integrity of his students. He returns again to *The Diviners* and the scene where Dan introduces Morag to his wife: "When students asked why would Dan bring Morag home and introduce her to his wife, I could deal with the question easily. If I didn't have joy and peace I couldn't have dealt with that question, except in an intellectual way, but I've come to terms with and grown in myself— and I've let go of fear. Students have huge dimensions to their questions and we need to respond as human beings first. You have to be real. You have to be able to put your cards on the table, to be nude, and then insist that students face themselves as clearly as possible and do the best they can.''

Where once he described himself as a frustrated actor, a teacher/actor ''subsumed by acting,'' he now sees himself as more like John Gielgud or Wayne Gretzky. He has achieved what he describes as ''distance, so you can move in and out. This is really important to get a handle on things so you can find a truer voice. The teacher's voice has to be cultivated and developed in such a way that we don't have to think, but we naturally say warm, encouraging things. Being able to do that comes from having inner peace.'' He returns again to the teacher as actor and the game image, which is very important to him. The classroom, he explains, ''is a game and we have to de-game the game. The frustrated actor can't de-game, because acting is a game. It's the caring person that makes it not entirely a game. Caring is what it's all about. The frustrated actor can't help kids go through the rites of passage. Kids attack authority figures as part of their way of establishing their identity, and teachers as authority figures have to be able to take it.

''You have to challenge yourself to behave in new ways,'' he concludes, ''and we need to challenge others to examine themselves.'' He believes that he has fought off all of his conditioned responses and describes himself now as unconventional. But he tries hard to make people who work in more conventional ways feel free and at ease with him. That is what he wants students to take away from or remember from his classes. He hopes that they will be able to say that in his classes they were in an environment where they could recondition responses, that in his classes there was ''a common search for understanding and a climate for open questions.'' In studying literature, he says, ''What's important is the kinds of contexts that are established and the discussions that are allowed.'' Ideally, for Raymond, the English curriculum would center on a search for meaning. He envisions the ideal setting this way: ''The classroom would be filled with walls of different books and students would embark on a search for meaning with materials I give them. Students would work together and determine what body of thought they want to work in. Teachers would work together in a team as resource people to motivate students and then push them along a joyful reading search of literature. Teachers would spend less time teaching and more time reading, sharing ideas, and looking for ways in which the mind can move one step forward. They would respond to students in caring and challenging ways and this manner of responding would be part of their total life—inside and outside the classroom. They would judge the quality and growth of students' thoughts and help them to understand the pain and joy of relationships, of family life—of life in general. Students would be given the freedom to explore, to learn to think, to write, and would leave as compulsive readers and writers.

"Content is very important, skills are important, and the intellect is important, but these are not the only thing," Raymond continues. "They won't go far if compassion, integrity, vision, and a love of learning aren't there." He cites as an example a former student who is now completing a Ph.D. in English. She is, as he describes her, a compulsive reader and writer, with a very sharp mind. "She is on an intellectual quest," he says. "But the intellect is not enough. It's just a tool. There should be a unity of mind, body, and soul. And she doesn't have that." He values the comments of those students who acknowledge how much they've learned about human interaction in his classes, and cites the example of one student who came to his twelfth-grade English class having never worked in groups or written anything longer than a paragraph. Raymond's response-centered classroom was an entirely new experience for her, and when he met her several years later in a shopping mall, he discovered that she had become a poetry reader. She read widely, reread the poetry they had studied in class, and also wrote poetry. Raymond concluded that this had happened because his classroom was not just a game. What happened in his classroom went far beyond that and had meaning for life. He acknowledges that the traditional teacher will also be able to recount success stories such as this, but feels strongly that it will happen much less frequently, "because kids in a collaborative setting are always forced into situations on their own."

Raymond is an enthusiastic and energetic proponent of his model of response teaching. For him, it is a whole way of being and of relating that comes, as he explains it, out of his sense of inner peace and joy, and at the same time it brings him joy and peace. He worries about the kind of teaching he used to do, but he runs into former students frequently and they reassure him that the seeds of what he is doing now were already there back then. He speaks of Glenda, a former student who still keeps in touch with Raymond whenever she returns to the city. She too reassured him on one of her recent visits that he "was the artist then, already bringing things together, getting them [students] to see things from different perspectives." And so he joyfully welcomes each new class because, as he explains, teaching is for him a continuation of his search for self.

In recounting the growth and development of their teaching dispositions, both Raymond and James cite the influences of their own past personal and professional experiences as having had powerful effects on their teaching practices. This echoes the findings of Butt, Raymond, and Townsend (1990). On the basis of their collection of more than 60 teacher autobiographies, they concluded that the "two most predominant categories of sources of influences that shape teacher development appear . . . to be the teacher's private life history and professional experience of teaching" (p. 10). Both James' and Raymond's stories center on these two categories. James dismisses formal educational training as having had no influence on his teaching practice, and in well over two years of conversations with me, Raymond does not even mention his teacher training. James and Raymond have distinctively different teaching styles, styles that reflect the unique individuality of each as a person. And although neither acknowledges a link between his formal teacher education and his present practice, there is considerable acknowledgment on the part of both teachers that their present practice has grown out of what Grumet (1988) describes as "the garden where [their] first worlds grew" (p. 191).

Raymond sees himself as having shed the cloak of his oppressive past and emerged as an entirely different kind of person and teacher. But in his interpretation and implementation of response teaching, he still retains many of the traits of his earlier, more directive approach, and his teaching continues to reflect the powerful influence of his stern, uncompromising, and rigidly structured home life.

Raymond rarely stands in front of the class to lecture. Most often his students are dispersed, divided into groups and working on their own, while Raymond moves from one group to the next, checking progress and telling students in response to their questions, "I don't interpret for you. I give context." It is unusual for him to assume a more traditional stance. When he teaches by telling or by lecturing, he tends to apologize for it. On one occasion, after teaching a class how to write business letters, Raymond says, "Sorry this is so traditional, but I do it because they've come back so often to tell me how useful this was." Raymond's classes appear to be very student-centered. Collaborative group work is the norm in his classes, the discourse patterns favor student–student exchanges, and the teacher is seen not at the front of the class, but standing at the side, encouraging the groups or reminding them of their tasks, but rarely dispensing information as the expert knower.

The new curriculum that Raymond has been implementing and promoting for a number of years focuses on the student as a learner, rather than on what is to be learned. It recognizes the importance of process in thinking and in communicating. It emphasizes students' responses to language and literature, and endorses an integrated approach to learning based on students exercising language skills through meaningful activities involving listening, speaking, reading, and writing. The new curriculum guide stresses the need for establishing a learning environment within which students can experience and use language in functional, artistic, and pleasurable ways. It is based on the belief that students need to use language in the classroom in order to take charge of their own learning, that language is a tool for learning, and that language users discover and give shape to what they know by using it. The curriculum guide encourages group activities as a means of facilitating learning and defines the role of the teacher as a coach, rather than as a purveyor of knowledge.

Barnes (1976), in distinguishing between transmission teaching and interpretive teaching, describes the interpretive teacher as one who:

1. Believes knowledge to exist in the knower's ability to organize thought and action,
2. Values the learner's commitment to interpreting reality, so that criteria arise as much from the learner as from the teacher,
3. Perceives the teacher's task to be the setting up of a dialogue in which the learner can reshape his knowledge through interaction with others,
4. Perceives the learner as already possessing systematic and relevant knowledge, and the means of reshaping that knowledge. (pp. 144–145)

Raymond's statements about his own beliefs and goals for teaching echo the criteria for interpretive teaching set forth by the new curriculum guide and by Barnes (1976). Raymond sees himself as a teacher of thinking, and maintains that his role is not to provide answers for students but to create an environment where thought and discussion are encouraged. He leaves questions open, frequently telling students to consider various possibilities or to go home and think about different interpretations. "Students," he says, "don't learn from what we tell them. They need to be given the freedom to explore—to learn to think. I refuse to work with definitive meanings because that destroys search." He wants his students to "explore different dimensions" and always to see the relationship between literature and life.

The casual observer in Raymond's classroom sees a student-centered environment, sees students listening to each other and interacting with each other as the teacher guide stands by on the side. A more probing examination of Raymond's practice, however, reveals that he has hardly relinquished the control he used to exercise when he taught in a more traditional teacher-centered style. He encourages the use of language, both oral and written, in order to learn, and there is a lot of active student involvement in his classes. However, by his own admission, it is not the students but he as the teacher who establishes the parameters of language usage and the types of activities in the class-room. Little is left to chance. Raymond determines the materials to be studied, the manner in which they are to be studied, and especially the time allowed for study. Only within these tightly controlled guidelines are students free to respond and engage in meaning-making discussions. Activities in Raymond's classes move very quickly. In one class, after spending the first hour having students act out the concept of irony, Raymond managed within the remaining seventeen minutes of class time to define irony, put the students into groups, read three poems, and have the groups decide on the type of irony found in each poem. Phrases such as "C'mon, move it," "You've got seven minutes," "Listen carefully. We haven't got much time," "Move quickly. Have one observation ready in about twenty seconds, a similarity or a difference," "I'll give you three minutes," and "What characterizes this style? Share in your groups. Talk about what you've written. I'll stop you in one minute," abound in his speech. He has trained his students well in the group process, and no time is wasted in the formation of groups and getting down to the task at hand. Raymond snaps out directions and claps his hands frequently to admonish those not on task, or to call attention to time. When he tells the class that they have four minutes or seven minutes within which to complete a task, that is precisely the amount of time they are given. He claps his hands, calls, "Time is up," and despite protests from students that they are not finished with their discussion or have not finished writing the number of pages he has assigned, Raymond moves on to the next activity. On occasion he interrupts a student in midsentence to announce that "It's the end of the class and there's no more time." Time drives the process in his classes and is as powerful a factor in his personal life as it is in his classroom. At the beginning of a new semester in January, as he outlines for a new class his expectations of them, he emphasizes the importance of planning and budgeting their time. He tells his students that being systematic and being able to plan and budget their time will guarantee them "on-the-job success." To illustrate, he recounts how through careful time management, he is able to fulfill the many demands on his personal and professional life. He tells his students that he is the president of a national organization, a full-time teacher, and the teacher of a church youth class, as well as a coach. He also spends 8 to 10 hours a week at his son's hockey practice. And he can get everything done because he plans ahead and uses his time wisely. He explains that he created the course outline they just received during the Christmas holidays. He does his marking while he waits at hockey practices, and if he cannot sleep at night, rather than lie in bed, he gets up and begins to work. Because he has planned in advance, he knows just what he should be working on, and consequently no time is wasted. In conclusion, he tells the group that "this emphasis on planning and time budgeting is one thing I'll hammer and hammer, one thing I'll observe." Then, because it is a new class, Raymond moves into a getting-acquainted exercise in which students walk about the room introducing themselves to those they don't know, and interviewing each other. Here as well, Raymond's instructions include the directive not to "spend too much time on one person, because you need to get to know everyone. You'll have to know each other by the end of the week, and I'll check not only if you know names, but you'll have to know something about the person."

Time, battling against time, budgeting time, and using time wisely are important elements in Raymond's life. They also figure prominently in the way he runs his classroom, and ultimately they affect the way in which his students encounter language and literature. There is no encouragement to linger over words or to savor images. Instead, in a briskly efficient, no-nonsense manner, Raymond directs students to:

> "Count up the soliloquies that precede and occur during or after each murder. You've got seven minutes."

> or

> "Decide in your groups very quickly what kind of irony it is."

> or

> "Let's take another four minutes to look at language."

> or

> "Think about whether there's one purpose or several. Does the style change? Don't bog down. Don't say I can't get through this. Force yourself. We're only going to be at this for another four or five minutes."

Raymond not only determines how much time is allotted for each activity, but also establishes the parameters for student responses by determining in advance that literature be studied from a social values perspective. He has said repeatedly that the process of "examining assumptions" and "reconditioning responses" has been of utmost importance to him in his life, and now he wants literature to be the vehicle for the same kind of self-revelatory process in his students' lives. Thus the focus in his classes is most often an examination of life, with literature acting as the springboard or catalyst for group discussions of the extra-textual. Through the questions he asks and the activities he assigns, he guides his students' initial responses to a text toward an examination of the connections between the events in literature and the events in their own lives. But Raymond moves through these response activities very quickly, controlling the type of response by the way in which he directs the students to focus on a text, and controlling the depth and breadth of the response by the time strictures imposed on the class. Seldom does a class discussion go beyond initial response to an interrogation of the text as Rosenblatt (1978) describes it, or move to the levels of interpretation or criticism as Scholes (1985) defines them. Raymond neither guides the class in this direction nor allows the class the time they would need to explore literature at these levels.

Raymond emphasizes in his classroom practice those elements that are important parts of his belief system and his personal life. Both time and the practice of examining life in order to restructure responses are of paramount importance to Raymond on a personal level, and they appear as critical elements of his professional practice. In a journal entitled "Musings on the Nature of Teaching," under the heading "Attitude of the Teacher," Raymond writes:

> It [the teacher's attitude] calls for compassion when the students take unexpected courses of action and reaction, when they need guidance and resent it, when they refuse cooperation, when they reach despair. . . . It calls for dedication to clarify parameters, verbalize assumptions and challenge philosophical positions without bringing undue hurt but with the willingness to hurt enough to bring passion to the search. It is a delicate balance which must be attempted and learned if real learning is to happen. Students must be challenged not just to learn course material but to live, not just to develop the intellect but also to develop better understanding of their feelings and the conditioned responses these feelings suggest. To cultivate only the mind is to cultivate the ingrown; to cultivate only feeling is to become narcissistic or sisyphistic; to cultivate both is to bring pride in self, joy in the accomplishments of others and an acceptance of the infinite as well as the finite.

Evidence of Raymond's need to structure and thereby control the learning environment of his classroom is found in the document he entitles "Principles of Learning." This is the course outline he gives to his students at the beginning of the second semester in which he describes the course as "student-centered, not teacher-centered," and identifies the teacher as the one who "creates contexts, works with process not content, and negotiates evaluation and grading." Although ostensibly a student-centered course, it is the teacher's outline that specifies for students what they will write, which materials they will read, when they will read them, and what questions they will answer. Each student must write one poem and one journal voice piece each week for 17 weeks. The folders containing this work will be called for without warning, and an incomplete folder will result in a mark of zero. In addition, the due dates for three drafts and the final submission of expository, persuasive, and entertaining paragraphs are also set forth in the outline. In literature as well, the themes chosen are those that figure prominently in Raymond's conversations and reflect his areas of interest and concern. The theme of relationships will be the focus for six weeks of study from February 1 to March 14. During this time various poems will be read, the short story to be studied will be "Mrs. Packletide's Tiger," the novel will be *Huckleberry Finn*, and the drama will be *Macbeth*. The formal essay assignment at the conclusion of the *Macbeth* study is a five-page paper on the topic "Macbeth: A potentially great man." The organization of this essay is to follow a specifically outlined pattern: "paragraph 1 = lead, paragraph 2 = thesis, paragraph 3 onward = development, and the last paragraph = conclusion." The next six-week period, from March 15 to May 2, is to be devoted to the theme of power. Several poems, "The Lottery," *1984*, and *A Doll's House* will be studied. This will then be followed by another six-week unit on the theme of love.

Raymond's strong belief in literature as a vehicle for teaching morals also harkens back to his past, to a religious upbringing in which the Bible was read frequently and its teachings guided all daily actions. Beyond the Bible, the only other reading material considered acceptable by his family was nonfiction of a didactic nature. It is the cloak of this "narrow, repressive, confining upbringing" that Raymond sought to shake. But the change in Raymond's teaching practice has not been as dramatic as he himself believes. He has not yet totally been able to project himself into the image of teaching that he describes as his ideal. As Briscoe (1990) suggests:

> . . . individual commitment to change on the part of a teacher is not sufficient to induce the desired changes. It is apparent that if changes are to occur in practices teachers must examine their beliefs, judgments, and thoughts regarding what they do and how they do it. Teachers need time to reflect on their own practices, assign language to their actions, and construct new knowledge which is consistent with the role metaphors they use to make sense of changes in their practice. (p. 16)

The metaphors that guide Raymond's practice today still revolve around control, the centrality of the teacher's role, and the power inherent in that role. In response to a request that Raymond list words, phrases, or ideas that come to mind when he reflects on the term "English teacher," he replies, "In teaching, the teacher is the text—in the McLuhan sense. The teacher is the message." He speaks often of having students find their voice, but at the same time Raymond likens himself to the conductor, the one who controls the voice. He refers to himself at various times as a shepherd, the students his flock, or as having to play God in the classroom, but nevertheless wanting "to exert the kind of compassionate authority that Moses and Abraham had."

As befits a student-centered, response-oriented teacher, Raymond encourages students to transact with the text and with each other. He seldom gives answers, but the questions he poses restrict the kinds of transactions that students can pursue, and shape the types of responses that will emerge. The first three of eight questions given to students studying *A Doll's House* were:

1. Will Helmer understand Nora? Write down "yes" or "no" and the reason.
2. Does Helmer really like Nora or not like her? Give a reason.
3. If your boyfriend/girlfriend said I'd like to sacrifice my life for you out of love, would you consider it love?

An eleventh-grade class studying *The Adventures of Huckleberry Finn* is told that "this breakdown of the novel is helpful if you don't read very well, or if you get bogged down. Using it is optional, but here it is: Chapter 1–7, 8–16, 17&18, 19–23, 24–30, 31, 32–43. Then answer the question 'To what other chapter is chapter 31 linked?'" A twelfth-grade class studying *The Diviners* is given an outline of the novel that traces the various themes, characters, and conflicts in the novel and provides page references to guide students' reading. Raymond had not provided guidelines for a novel study earlier in the year and felt that this "lack of parameters left some of them floundering."

Shortly before exams, which are prepared by the English teachers in the school, Raymond sets out to prepare his students for writing them. He is aware that in this context, his teaching is more overtly directive and he apologizes, saying, "This isn't response teaching as I'd like to see it, but the reality of exams only three weeks away. I've got to prepare them for the demands of exam questions by giving them practice in exam-type responses." Students are told that the exam will be worth approximately one-third of their final mark, and his intent is to have them work through some possible exam questions. As the first practice piece, students are given a poem and told to comment on the use of diction, imagery, rhythm, and rhyme. After students have spent a few minutes writing answers, Raymond calls, "Stop. Which words have you discussed?" One student responds by telling him what ideas she has gleaned from the poem, but he interrupts her, saying, "I asked which words." He goes on to tell his students that "There are four ways of examining a poem: paraphrase, thematic, allegory, and a problem-solving approach. Make sure you have the literal meaning first, and make sure your evidence is rooted in the text. If you've got an unorthodox interpretation, couch it as a possibility, not as the meaning."

A student interjects: "I thought you were supposed to say what you think it means to you and that's what it is."

But Raymond doesn't respond to her challenge; he merely tells the class, "Okay. You've got seven minutes. Please write."

Then, as a form of exam preparation for possible *Hamlet* questions, Raymond gives the class the following assignment: "Hamlet is a clever but muddled man. You have ten minutes to write a page." When they have finished writing, Raymond tells the class that all exam questions for *Hamlet* are the same. They center either around his emotions or his clever mind. He asks the students to cite those scenes that could be used in support of an "emotions" question and those scenes that could be used to support a "clever mind" question. Michael, who didn't quite manage to jot down all the scenes according to their categories, asks, "Which scenes did you say showed his clever mind?" To which Raymond, shying away from the role of transmitter of information, responds: "I didn't say that. You said that as a class." Then he goes on to tell the class, "Another trick for exams—be organized and be specific about scenes and words. Work your strengths for three or four pages. Talk about what you know, and then say, 'Time doesn't permit the discussion of _____,' and then mention the things you can't do or don't know anything about, in a well-structured phrase. Give the impression that you know and the examiner will be left with the impression that you know."

A student asks, "Would you be fooled?"

Raymond replies, "I'd give you credit for having brains. Exams are a game. Treat them that way."

After the class is over, Raymond comments that he used to teach like this, in a more frontal, teacher-directed way, but is glad that he doesn't anymore. With reference to exams he repeats again, "Exams are a game, so you do what you can to teach them a few tricks." He recounts his own high school experience with grade twelve English. He failed the final exam four times, and after three years, on his fifth attempt, he scored 81 percent. The reason he passed then, he says, is because a teacher in the summer school that he attended spent four days teaching him how to pass an exam. That is why he does the same thing with his students now.

In these exam preparation classes, Raymond acknowledges his teacher-centered approach. Although the outer trappings of teacher-centeredness are not readily apparent in his other classes, he nevertheless maintains the same tight control, channeling activities toward the kind of literature study that he is comfortable with—literature for life. Structure and control figured prominently throughout Raymond's youth—at home, at school, in the church, and in the community. Upon becoming a teacher, he modeled himself after a very controlling professor and lived his personal life according to the rules imposed by the rigid structures of his family's and his community's religious beliefs. He has struggled against his past, has fought to restructure his thinking and to recondition his responses. Structure and control were the significant elements highlighted in Raymond's accounts of memorable biographical incidents, and despite his struggles they remain the significant elements in his teaching practice today. Although the outer manifestations of his practice have changed, the need to function as the dominant and controlling figure in the classroom still manifests itself in Raymond's questions to students, in his language, in his metaphors, in his use of time, and in his choice of activities and assignments. As Thomas' (1989) epigraph in *Latakia* contends, ''All human beings tend to keep to the old ways even when they are adding the new.''

Similarly to James' teaching, there is a consistency evident throughout the span of Raymond's teaching practice. Clandinin (1986) addresses this theme of consistency in teacher practice. Zeichner and Tabachnik (1985), Britzman (1986), Grumet (1988), Bullough (1990), Knowles and Ems (1990), and Butt, Raymond, and Townsend (1990) note that these coherent practices are strongly rooted in the teachers' biographies. The findings of Olson's (1980) study serve to illustrate Clandinin's (1986) argument (referred to in Chapter 2) and clearly parallel the developments in Raymond's teaching. The starting point of Olson's (1980) study was the problem of implementation of new curricula. Olson, working with eight science teachers who were implementing a new curriculum, found that the most important underlying construct in their implicit theories of teaching was classroom influence. However, the new science curriculum being implemented at the time of the study called for reduced teacher influence in the classroom. According to Olson's analysis, the teachers dealt with the tension between their belief that teacher influence should be high and the curriculum developer's belief that teacher influence should be low by adapting the curriculum project so that it became compatible with the teachers' implicit theories of good teaching. Olson (1980) concluded:

> In short, after a period of experimentation during which they saw their influence declining, the teachers re-established influence through varied domestications of the project doctrine. (p. 265)

Raymond's response to a new approach in curriculum has been precisely as Olson (1980) and Clandinin (1986) define it. He has domesticated the concepts of a new teaching model in such a way as to make them compatible with his own needs for structure and control, and through this adaptation has ensured the coherence and consistency of his practice.

Holland (1968, 1975) speaks of this same coherence from the perspective of literary theory, and I believe that a parallel can be drawn between the reader transacting with a text and the teacher responding to a curriculum document. According to Holland, literary interpretation is a function of identity. Readers respond to a literary work by projecting onto it and by taking from it that which is compatible with the reader's identity theme. If readers respond positively to a work or to parts of it, it is because they can construe events in the text in such a way as to be compatible with and fulfill the needs of their own identity themes. Alternatively, if readers have no reactions to a literary work, or a negative one, then they haven't been able to incorporate or adapt the work in such a way as to be compatible with their personal themes. Readers thus re-create texts, as it were, according to their own personalities. Implicit in Holland's model is the notion that individuals have a central identity theme that remains constant throughout their lives. Although there may be variations on the central theme and it may be expressed differently, nevertheless it manifests itself in all aspects of a person's life. Holland (1975) maintains that we can ascertain a person's identity theme by searching out the patterns of repetition, contrast, modulation, structure, and mission in the details of an individual's behavior. The identity theme can be abstracted from this behavior in the same way that a central theme can be established to express the unity of all the many words in a literary work. Holland's basic principle of the act of reading is that readers take what they read as the raw material from which to create one or more variations of their continuing identity theme. Readers will read differently because they have different personalities, but always the reading response will be defined by the reader's own identity theme.

In their study, Butt, Raymond, and Yamagishi (1988) also draw attention to the concepts of unity and consistency. After studying a number of teachers' autobiographical accounts, they concluded that teacher knowledge and teacher practices are "grounded as much, if not more so, in life history than just current contexts and action. . . . " (p. 151). In their interpretation of the stories written and told by Lloyd, one of the teachers in their long-term study, Butt et al. (1988) conclude that:

> Lloyd's early life (persons, experiences, family) are the ultimate roots of Lloyd's thoughts and actions. Later, professional influences, academic knowledge and experience serve mainly as substance into which he infuses his personal knowledge from the early years into his form of professional knowledge. (p. 143)

Just as Holland (1975) refers to variations on a central theme of behavior, Butt et al. (1988), in tracing the development of Lloyd's teaching practice, also conclude that:

> Lloyd's professional development mainly involves incremental elaboration of original patterns. In a sense, we see the domination of his professional knowledge by his private architecture of self. (p. 143)

The theme of approval as a recurring motif in Raymond's story serves to illustrate further Holland's (1975) contention of an underlying consistency, with variations on a theme, and Butt et al.'s (1988) claim of the process of "incremental elaboration of original patterns" (p. 143). In recalling his youth and family life, Raymond speaks of trying to win his father's approval and recounts an incident on the farm when he devised a work method that proved to be more time-efficient than the method his father used. But to Raymond's disappointment, his father neither acknowledged the superiority of Raymond's innovation nor approved of any changes to the usual routine. In the matter of choosing a career, Raymond was strongly influenced by Elaine's disapproval of law as a profession. But his subsequent choice, teaching, met with the approval of both his family and his community. As a beginning teacher, his students' approval was very important to him, and he concedes that initially he structured his classroom in such a way as to become the focal point, the center, of his students' attention, approval, and admiration. He notes that he became depressed when his popularity waned after changing from a teacher-centered to a student-centered teaching approach. Now, however, he feels that he has achieved what he describes as "a distancing," and consequently is no longer troubled by diminished student attention or acclamation. Although Raymond can accommodate the fact that he no longer has the star status he once enjoyed in the classroom, this need is met in different ways now. His need for approval is still apparent in the stories he recounts of former students who return to praise him for his teaching, of new acquaintances who applaud his methods, of teachers who come to visit and learn from him, of university professors who videotape his classes, and of international associations that invite him to speak at their conferences. His star status has shifted from the classroom to a much larger stage, and confirmation of his worth comes from other areas now.

At the classroom level, Raymond's need for approval, his need to be right, is still evident in his relationship with his students. Although he invites and encourages their responses, wants them to become independent learners, his own reaction to students' ideas or questions that challenge his authority is much the same as his father's response was to him so many years ago. In one class devoted to business writing, Raymond lists the elements of effective business writing and then focuses on precise language usage. To illustrate, he tells the class not to use a phrase such as "burst into the room" because "burst" has two meanings. Ben challenges this pronouncement, but Raymond doesn't allow him the time to develop his argument or continue a discussion. Instead, he presents a scenario to the class and asks them to write a letter to a car repair shop, requesting compensation for shoddy workmanship. "The amount of money you ask for is determined by the validity of your argument," he tells the class. And the format they are to use "breaks the letter into three distinct parts with separate headings: summary, request, and background." He explains how they are to write and then says, "Let's try to complete this in twenty minutes. You can do it in partners. I'll go up and down the rows to check progress." In response to a student's question of "Why can't I do it my way?" he answers that this is a format that has proven to be successful and therefore they should follow it. The class begins the letters, but questions continue to arise because students are not sure of how to apply the format to their writing. Raymond says, "Let's talk about this a little more. Who's got paragraph one written?" Christine reads hers, but she has begun with background. Raymond tells her that she cannot start with background. "The test is, what do you want?"

Christine replies, "I want money."

"Then start your letter off that way," he tells her. "Ask for the money first."

Another student interjects, "But you can't start off with that. If I got a letter like that I'd be insulted."

A discussion ensues as to the correctness of this approach, and Raymond eventually says, "Why argue? This works."

Graham, still not convinced, says, "You're asking me to change something I've done successfully in another way."

"How successfully?" Raymond asks as he reads Graham's letter, pointing to what he considers the weaknesses in it. But then he says, "All right. Go with it. I'm just giving you some examples of what works." Although Raymond gives Graham permission to proceed in his own way, his final statement, as well as all of the preceding discussion, is tinged with doubt that anything except his assigned three-part format can be effective.

Raymond deems it important that his students accept and approve of his specific classroom procedures, and recounts with pride stories of those outside the classroom who have also endorsed his methods. He tells of a business executive whom he encountered on an overseas flight. They shared stories, and Raymond reports that the executive went away impressed with what Raymond was doing in his classes, saying that his company was working with their employees in much the same way. Raymond's stories of former students almost always center on the students' strong support and approval of his new teaching style. His own endorsement of the new curriculum, with its student-centered emphasis, and his adoption of the currently popular language of response teaching ensured for Raymond the approval of those in the forefront of the new movement in language arts education. And although a well-respected colleague in the student-centered collaborative learning research project in which Raymond was involved expressed reservations about Raymond's interpretation of student-centered teaching, Raymond dismisses these reservations as coming from a man who really "doesn't know, because he's not in school every day." Instead he points to the supportive comments of a university professor who visited his class one day and left at the end of it, as Raymond reports, excited and enthusiastic, saying that he had "never seen anything like it" and that "it was an incredible experience."

As Holland (1975) suggests, the theme of approval, though varied in its manifestations, can be abstracted from Raymond's story by searching out, within the details of the classroom observations and the biographical incidents that he brings to the fore, the patterns of repetition, contrast, modulation, and adaptation. And just as Butt et al. (1988) conclude that Lloyd's professional development is dominated by his private architecture of self and characterized by incremental elaboration of original patterns, Raymond's teaching practice too can be seen as a complex weave that carries the recurring traces of his past, a past which continues to color and shade his present actions.

Chapter 4

The Pain of Visibility: Raymond's Response

James' and Raymond's stories as they appear in the last two chapters are abbreviated versions of the reports that I gave to each of the teachers. At regular intervals throughout the period of our work together, both teachers had received my observational notes so that they might corroborate my observations, make comments, and raise questions. Although their written responses to these fieldnotes were not nearly as lengthy or detailed as I had initially expected they would be, the observations recorded in my notes often acted as a starting point for our conversations when next we met. In our conversations we talked about emerging themes and tentative interpretations, and when I reached the final writing stage, both teachers received drafts of each portion of the report as I completed it. James made only a few comments about the writing and corrected some errors of grammar. Raymond declined to read the drafts. He was very busy and preferred to talk about the contents, saving the reading for the end, when he had the whole document before him. When the report was completed, James was quite comfortable with what he found on its pages. Raymond was not and responded very strongly.

Raymond called me immediately after he had read the completed report. He seemed calm on the telephone, but he was clearly unhappy with what he had just read. He said, "It's true, but that's not how I want to see myself." I didn't realize the extent of his unhappiness, though, until a few days later when he brought me his journal, into which he had poured the anguish he felt.

Completing the written report of our study and handing it to Raymond signaled to me the end of the project, and the end of nearly three years of work together. But I was soon to return to the project because of Raymond's response. We began to meet again to discuss how the research had affected Raymond, what we might learn from our work together, how we might have conducted ourselves differently, and how we might bring our experience to a larger audience of researchers working in the schools. It was because of our long-term professional relationship that I had been able to gain access to so much of Raymond's teaching world. It was also within this relationship that our problems centered. But now it was also precisely because of our professional relationship and the respect that had developed between us that we were able to deal with the issue at hand in a forthright manner. We reopened the story, stepped back from what we had done, viewed it critically, and began again to write and record our thoughts and questions as we entered into a new collaborative phase of inquiry.

This new phase of inquiry began as a result of Raymond's journal, and he agreed that it should be included in the book. What follows are his thoughts as he set them down over a period of three days after reading the full report for the first time. As a way, possibly, of distancing himself from the painful experience of reading about himself, Raymond wrote most of his response in the third person. Throughout his journal response he referred to me as Sheila, and retained for himself the pseudonym Raymond, which we had used in the report to ensure his anonymity. Other than some grammatical editing and the removal of place names, here are Raymond's words.

May 7, 6:00 P.M.

Raymond sits on a kitchen chair. He is exhausted. He nibbles at some supper. The phone has been ringing off the hook—players wanting to know when the next practice is. Finally, all is quiet. His eyes focus on the folder of some 200 pages on the kitchen table. He doesn't want to read it. Too tired. But he should. At least some of it. He examines the table of contents, flips to page 93—predictably—and reads Sheila's summary of her impressions of him as a teacher and, supposedly, person. Almost immediately he senses here a piece of writing he wished he wouldn't need to read. Words such as "Raymond *warned*," "moved *briskly*," "asking *quick* questions and waiting only for *brief* responses," "*holds up* the page that he has written and *directs* the students," words that echo frenzy and superficiality. This is exactly what he doesn't want to be. His exhaustion has receded somewhat. He must read on, a kind of walking of a phosphoric gauntlet. He must reassure himself with thoughts of other times—students like Jeff, who had dropped English several times and were giving it one more try; like Natalie, who struggled with suicide and had always hated school; and so on and so on. He remembered that these people had been left to drift in so many other classrooms, that they couldn't structure their time and their living. And he asked himself—did he have a choice if he wanted all students to have the opportunity of doing their best? It would have been so easy just to let these people falter and work with the Andys and the Joyces, young people who would succeed even if teachers floated. And so phrases like "He could be a good teacher only if he *imposed* [himself] on the learning" stung, as did the incoherent sequencing of statements—from "imposed . . . on learning" . . . to . . . "uneasiness" . . . to "akin to artist's." How could he be so incoherent? Was he really that way? This was so very painful. He tried to reassure himself that whatever he had done in his classes, it had always been his passion that all students be given an equal opportunity, and that he had felt the control had been needed to make certain that not only those who wanted to learn could, that all would be given equal opportunity. And even though he felt these thoughts mere, illusory, suave, they were all he could find in this moment. And then had he used the word *girls* to refer to female students? A word he now finds so offensive? Anyhow, it hurt to see it quoted as his word.

   The reading brings him increasing distress, especially when he reads that he has referred to his own teaching as "response teaching" and Sheila says he has "*molded* . . . approach . . . been part of . . . into uniquely his own." She goes on to say that "because Raymond is not . . . familiar with Rosenblatt or other response theorists, he defines the term in his own way, . . . with a heavy emphasis on the role of the teachers and the teacher's response to students, as *opposed* to an emphasis on the response to text." Had he really deemphasized reading and thinking about text when he was so concerned that students learn to speak with each other, everyone speak with each other, that cliques not have a forum in the classroom? He couldn't understand this now. Wasn't it rather the opposite; namely, that as students learned to care about each other, everyone in the classroom caring about everyone else in the classroom, was it not then that far more serious so-called "interrogations" of text could take place? He had thought so then; now he felt he had simply missed the mark. Who has the right to define "response teaching" once and forever? He felt as if he had defiled a sacred movement. He asked, "How can a way of living and relating to others" be at variance with response to text when the response literature of the Smiths and the Rosenblatts and the many others he has read since this time constantly talk about the voice of the reader as part of the meaning of the text? Is the text not read with much more understanding when students feel increasingly free to share their biases with those with whom they read? Pain. Pain. And more pain.

   He wants only to sleep, but he cannot. He reads on—"On one occasion where the discussion *'centers on life issues, which Raymond favors'* it ends with a discussion about student behavior in groups.'' This sounds as if text is unimportant. He winces. Did Sheila not know that this was preparation for discussion of Macbeth as a tragic person rather than as a cold-blooded murderer or as someone who meets the criterion of an Aristotelian definition? Anyone reading this would surely think Raymond merely a moralist or possibly even some classroom voyeurist. The sting deepens. He begins to despair.

And then ''he sees himself more like a Gielgud or Wayne Gretzky.'' How does a paragraph on the nature of ''distance'' link with these two? He rereads. The link seems not to be there. He had meant that he had observed these two closely, had seen the distance they were able to live in the midst of the passionate moment, and had asked if this capacity in their roles as actor and athlete could help him and his students to acquire this in reading, writing, and living. Anyone reading this paragraph could only assume a troubled and arrogant Raymond using the classroom as a forum for frustration. And maybe that was all he had ever been, but it wasn't what he had tried to be.

And finally, when he speaks of an ideal classroom, ''The classroom . . . filled with walls of different books where students would embark on a search of meaning with materials *I give them.*'' Not only wordy, inaccurately expressed, but also arrogant and controlling. How could he have said that? ''I give,'' especially when he had been so committed to student choice in reading for the general courses in English since the fall of 1972. He had had an extensive classroom library during the seventies, long before it had become the movement it became in the eighties and nineties. The library had slowly died because the school refused money for classroom libraries. He would buy $100 worth of books with his own money; too little to keep it growing; only enough to give nonreaders a start. Students had always designed their own reading and writing programs, leaving him all his time to help students with their writing and with discussion about their reading. It had been this that had led so many students to move from the general to the more academic English classes and do well. These students could spend all their time reading and writing; he, all his time helping. Classroom talk had not been a focus then. He remembers how students turned off school would start with *Run Shelley Run*, and dozens of books later, would read *East of Eden* in one weekend, or start with *The Outsiders* and end with *Clockwork Orange* or *One Flew Over the Cuckoo's Nest* or *1984*. How could he have said *I give them?* And so the pain.

And he muses further. How much he had wanted to open up the reading of at least the novel in the academic English courses, but the pressure from the school to prepare students for conventional, lit crit exams as well as a community that wanted students to receive the course everyone else got was simply too strong for him to challenge. And so he had allowed choices, as many as four novels for each unit. As he mused, it struck him that the class Sheila had observed was the one course he had not had time to revamp, that he had taught as he had seven years earlier. That it had also been a class with so many troubled students had forced him to teach in ways he had always resented. And now, it was this class which had served as the sample. Why, why only this class, a class with six students whom no one else in the English Department wanted to teach? Why, it kept echoing around and around in his head.

He couldn't read on. He was most upset. Couldn't think or eat or even talk much. All that he had striven not to be, he still was, at least if this account meant what it seemed to mean. That night he slept with the help of tranquilizers. What would his friend James think of him? Would he really only see this frenetic, insensitive moralist? He hoped not, but he couldn't see it otherwise.

Next morning he wanted to get to work early, but he couldn't. That folder on the kitchen table, like a flame to a moth. When everyone had left for school, he began to read again. He read until 10:30. The horror he had felt the night before became increasingly graphic. Questions to *A Doll's House*—1) . . . 2) . . . 3) . . . Sheila writes: "The questions he poses restrict . . . transactions." Oh, God. Not that class, where, according to SAT scores, student reading levels range from grade 3 to grade 12, the one with foreign students whose English language skills were so very weak. And why would Sheila not also mention the other half of that course, where students had devised their reading and writing programs?

So many frustrating moments. Sheila writes that "although he invites and encourages their responses . . . his own reaction to students' ideas or questions that challenge his authority is much the same as his father's response was to him many years ago." He is puzzled. How could anyone say that after watching him in plenary sessions where students were talking about a text such as a poem, especially when observers had seen this discussion with a range of classes including the enriched and the work experience classes? How could this be possible? The subsequent example brought the evidence. Business writing. This part of the course for this class could take forever if one wanted to do so using a response model. Maybe he shouldn't

even have taught it. It was meant to give students some strategies
should they have need to write request, complaint, cover letters,
progress reports, proposals and evaluation reports, etc. Business writing in other classes included merely a general business letter and
maybe a resume. Raymond just couldn't see the relevance of this example to illustrate betrayal of response learning. And where was
Sheila during the part of the course when students went on from
these three directed classes to choose an area of research and to prepare a major proposal or evaluation report to the insurance company
about the unfairness of auto insurance, or to the City Council about
Heritage Homes or zoning by-laws; reports with dozens of appendi-
ces, countless sources including primary as well as secondary; classes
where researching, reading, writing, constant talk prodded the
search for meaningful communication? Why would she use an isolated example to make the case that Raymond was not what he pro-
fessed to be, at least not according to the theorists? It really hurt.

With this despair he turned to Sheila's discussion of James. The
tone is so much different. It is relaxed. She quotes James in phrases
like ''A good teacher is one who can express things clearly and is patient enough to work with individuals.'' This is beautiful. There is
peacefulness in Sheila's recall of the link James makes between *Julius
Caesar* and the Armenians in Azerbaijan. It is all so peaceful. Raymond had tried to do these things when he came from his last school
to the present one in 1971. He was driven to drink. It was all he could
do to survive that year. He tried it several times in subsequent years
but always with equal disaster. And yet this is all he had done in his
last school—make these links for students. They seemed to like it. In
this school he had very few students in the lower streams whose attention span exceeded five minutes. Why am I raising this? I don't
know except that it hurts that everything Raymond has striven to do
to free students is seen as a betrayal of response learning and that everything James does is seen as sensitive and a meaningful move from
traditional to response teaching. It is as if I am on trial for my beliefs
and aspirations and James is not, that the peacefulness of James'
words, his quiet manner with students, that these make his confessed traditional role warm and wonderful. And it is. I admire it. But
when he meets students who want to stage a play after school and on
Saturday mornings, where are the references to the hours Raymond
spent with debaters and public speaking participants; ones who went
on to win national championships, and did so largely on the skills
they developed talking about literature in their groups? Raymond
couldn't meet students Saturday mornings because his commitments

to community clubs and home didn't allow it, though he had done so constantly during the years before his children were born. It is wonderful that James does this. It illustrates that he cares. The problem with Raymond was that he too spent hours doing things for kids because he cared, but we see only the autocrat who merely shifts settings. It really hurts.

That brings to mind Sheila's claim that Raymond left center stage in his classroom—though little evidence exists that this is in fact so—and shifted it to the national and international stage. This may be true on the surface. But is there no room with such theories for thoughtful consideration? Does she know how much Raymond tried not to do the national keynote address, how he worked 60 hours to speak 15 minutes? Does she not know that he refused several times to allow his nomination as vice-president of a national association, but that once he had taken the task, he felt he should do the best he could? It was hard and often agonizing to do good work. And so, on and on. He did not create the world stage. Even more, he gave up the classroom stage long before embarking on the provincial, national, and world stage. It hurts that the only explanation is the one Sheila gives, an explanation which describes a child in need of territory. Did she ask Raymond's students and colleagues about this need to be center stage? Or people with whom he works at the national and international levels? Or the woman he is married to? Or his children? Certainly he tries to please people, but can that not also be because he wants to do his best, wants those with whom he works to feel the special love he has for them? It hurts to be seen as a manipulator.

It reminds him of a parallel. Just as the detail used to gossip can also be used to acquire compassionate understanding of others, so cannot events that peacock some to superficial prominence be events that for others are an expression of the most distilled, sacrificial love? If this is not possible, then Raymond must ultimately despair, or he must breathe the thoughts of a Sir Thomas More when he says to Margaret in response to her statement—"Then if you elect to suffer for it, you elect yourself a hero" that "Why then perhaps we must stand fast a little—even at the risk of being heroes." Why must an interpretation of others always necessarily follow prescribed theories of psychology? Raymond does not say Sheila is necessarily wrong; he does want more evidence that her theory is true. Everything about James is gentleness. That is also why Raymond likes him so much. But is there no gentleness in Raymond? Anywhere?

Sheila makes much of James' knowledge of the world. That is wonderful. Raymond envies this. But Raymond's knowledge isn't ex-

actly limited. When Sheila asked him whether he read much, Raymond remembers it was in the staff room, and that in the heat of that moment thought of reading the novels and the books of theorists in education. Naturally he said he didn't read enough. But to read few novels doesn't say a person isn't a reader. Since 1975 he had always read *English Quarterly* and *English Journal*—from cover to cover, had read Moffett and Britton. His general-level writing courses were modeled in large part on *Writing Narrative—And Beyond* (Dixon & Stratta). He could think of many others he had read over the years. And poetry. He had always subscribed to *Currents in Poetry*, had bought and read all the poetry books published by Wordwise Press, had come to love Ondatji's *Billy the Kid* and Cooley's *Bloody Jack*. And so many more. Why would Sheila not have asked this on another occasion? Sure he should have known better than to say he didn't read much, that he was too busy. But this just wasn't really true. And magazines. These he still reads between periods at hockey games. And who else anywhere was as concerned about the need for female main characters and female writers balancing the high school literature courses loaded with authors and main characters who were white and European? Raymond had balanced courses with these considerations as early as 1974. He had enormous respect and love for literature. But did it also need to emerge in every class he taught? Did it need to emerge at all? Was it not enough to let students examine the texts on their own—the richness of all four of Margaret Laurence's Manawaka novels, the language of a Brook or of a Stacey? Is the only way to *lead*, as she keeps saying James does, to tell students? Is that the only way to help students appreciate words? Is there no room for students to explore these on their own as they always did sometime during the study?

This might well sound like defense. It is not meant to be. It is meant to ask the question—Why does Raymond never quite reach the standards Sheila says "student-centered" classrooms ought to have? This is a negative. References to James are always a positive, or at least placed in a context to make them seem positive. Where Raymond is frenetic, James is calm; where Raymond never reads, James always reads; where Raymond is the autocrat, James is the negotiator. Why the polarities? Is there no grey here? Are the degrees of each not determined by setting, imagination, and energy?

It is interesting that nothing is said about writing; either about student writing or about teacher writing. Nor is anything said about the strategies used to help students with their writing. She says that with Raymond writing is always hurried. Do theorists not allow for

such writing to prompt thought? Did she not see the reading logs written by students in the advanced and general classes during their reading of novels? Why would she not want to examine the hours in which students helped each other and in which Raymond helped students with their transactional and poetic writing? Instead she merely lists the assignments and the dates on which they are due; all the clinical stuff which all too often was changed because students needed them changed.

She says that "he encourages the use of language . . . however, by his own admission, it is not the students, but he . . . who establishes the parameters of language usage and types of activities. . . . Raymond determines the materials to be studied, the manner in which they are to be studied, and especially the time allowed for study." This was true to a large degree with the classes Sheila refers to. But what about the enriched course where students were given considerable choice of material, where they decided whether they would write research papers, novellas, or books of poetry? Sheila is correct about the eleventh-grade academic class she observed and about the portion of the eleventh-grade general class she observed. But this is not the whole picture. Does "student-centered" have only one definition? Is there no range or degree depending on class makeup, community expectation, school climate? That Raymond insisted he was student-centered and that this was untrue if one uses Rosenblatt's definition of "interrogating the text" is true in some, maybe many, instances in these two difficult classes. But does that mean he doesn't measure up? Is there no room for approximation? It is also true that he was less aware of his work than he is now, that he now realizes he was on a scale, but it is also true that the scale depended on the type of class, the time available, and the energy he could give it. To have given more choice to the eleventh-grade academic class Sheila so often saw was to invite disaster, given the way the course was set up. As earlier stated, there hadn't been time and energy to revise it. Only six or so students in the class could have coped with more decisionmaking, given the conditions.

And then Raymond's belief in literature as "a vehicle for teaching morals," the phrase pains. Margaret Laurence says in the National Film Board production about her life that every serious novelist is also a moralist. The key word is *also*. Is it moralistic to ask students to link their own experience to literature before discussion focuses on the structure of the novel or poem or play? Is someone who uses literature not one who teaches fiction as a recipe book for what is right and wrong about life? Maybe Raymond had his definitions confused,

but if he did, can it not also be questioned that theorists define words into meaningless definitions, meaningless because they fail anymore to describe what is happening? The references to *A Doll's House* (eleventh-grade general class with the range of students), *Huck. Finn* (eleventh-grade academic class with all the problem students), and to *Diviners* (twelfth-grade academic class) where the sheet of page numbers was merely a guide for those who wanted to use it. Students most often ignore it.

May 8

Still in despair, he read the first 71 pages. He felt much better. Sheila had avoided jargon, had struggled with the dilemma she faced in this task—how to be fair and representative at the same time. He felt good about this reading.

He decided to reread the narratives of James and himself against this background. He felt better than the day before when he had read these stories in isolation. But the sorrow set in once more. If he were someone choosing between James and Raymond, he would never choose Raymond. In James' class he as student could learn if he wanted to, could get reprieves if he didn't get his work done, wouldn't need to write often, and above all, he could sit and take it in. He would never choose frenetic Raymond with all the pressure to get things done. And even if he loved to talk, the way Raymond's story is written, the talk would never be more than mere chatter.

And so he went to bed once more grieving that he ever got himself into this.

May 9

Raymond recalls the realization of the point she wishes to make; namely, that teacher change is influenced considerably by the background they bring to their teaching; especially the way teachers have grown up in their families and the way they have been taught by their teachers, is clear. It is also clear that what teachers say about themselves is not necessarily what happens. This has been known for a long time; her thesis has reinforced this.

However, several questions remain.

First, the way it is written wouldn't matter if James and Raymond didn't know each other so well. It would be a usual intellectual exercise—no implications for life. In this instance, James, a classroom teacher, is left with all the cards; Raymond, who is hired to help

teachers change, is left with a serious credibility problem. Because the paper refuses to allow degrees within the definition of response teaching, it finds him not only lacking, but also someone to whom truth is not important. The paper does not take into account either degree or the circumstance within which he has worked.

Second, it raises the whole question of whose voice do we have here. Is it the speaker who understands response theory from the books she has read? Is it also the author who brings with her a whole set of baggage of which neither Raymond or James know? Raymond wonders why every time he trusts women who come from his own cultural background he is always regarded as less than sincere. Is there something about this cultural background that makes women mistrust men? Are the men unusually paranoid, and is he one of those? Why does it seldom, almost never happen with women who do not come from this background? This raises the third dimension of voice. Is the audience unable to read in this instance? Is Raymond's perceiving sufficiently paranoid to make careful reading of this paper impossible? Is he so used to adulation that when he faces censure he cannot face life? Is what he considers censure here not really censure but an attempt to force a thesis into consistency, i.e., was it necessary to select information which would suit the development of the thesis even at the expense of the way things really are and the reasons why they are so? Presently he feels he has been judged without recourse to dialogue before the verdict. It is true that Sheila showed him his narrative, but without the backdrop of James' story, and, with the unusual trust he had in Sheila, he didn't, or couldn't, read then as he reads now.

The argument is not that the thesis isn't true, i.e., that the way people teach is influenced more by background than by teacher education. The argument is that a formula was imposed; that isolated and peripheral classroom incidents were used to make all-inclusive generalizations; that Raymond had to measure up and James didn't.

May 10, 12:00 Noon

Really enjoyed the dance last night. Elaine and I hadn't danced for a long time. It was so wonderful. To dance is to make poetry and music. It patterns us into new ways of feeling and being.

I also taught my usual tenth-grade Sunday school class, a job I've done for 17 years, every year wanting to quit, every year solicited back in by the end of September. But it felt good. Helped me believe that I do allow others to think and to feel free to speak. Discussion

centered on Mother's Day, that every day should be Mother's Day in
the sense that we take our turns at the work mothers must usually
do; that love comes in different forms; that it is easy to romanticize
but not so easy to be honest and to sacrifice; that commitment comes
in degrees and approximations even though it is total in each case—
only the parameters and capacity to love vary, etc. When we talked
about graduation, they wanted to know if we could continue these
discussions next year. It reassured me somewhat that maybe Raymond wasn't as bad as the thesis had made him out to be. I thought
of the comment that Raymond's classes don't allow for "interrogation" of the text. As I listened to these young people examine the
words "love" and "commitment," I couldn't help but ask if this
wasn't a rather serious interrogation of these words and their texts. It
also made me ask if text is only the written word before us. In my
reading of Rosenblatt last summer I felt strongly that text included
much more than just the words on the page, that it could include the
setting in which the words are read, the baggage readers bring to
these words, etc. In short, to "interrogate" can mean bringing all
these factors into play.

Interesting how Sheila's thesis preoccupied me when I showered
this morning, during the class and again now. Maybe this will be a
growing time for me even if it means losing credibility with James
and others who work with him. Raymond has little problem with the
notion that he imposed himself on much of the learning. He has
much problem with the way the thesis does it.

I have just reread page 126, a page I turned to at random. It
pains me to reread it. Doesn't seem to matter which page I turn to or
when I do so, the pain gets worse as I read. I really must stop and
just forget this.

This journal continues to ramble. I suppose it reflects the pain of
it all. I realize that nothing I write will do more than help me cope.

Another recall. Use of classroom drama. Raymond uses improvi-
sation. It is rooted in life. James' use of drama is always rooted in
text. A possible reason for this has been discussed elsewhere. But
that Raymond never roots drama in text illustrates again the limited
view Sheila has of Raymond. Where was she during times when soliloquies were read by three students and their readings examined for
the meaning each provided? When students presented poems,
scenes from novels? All this is peripheral to the thesis she develops
but central to the honesty with which portraits are given.

I've got to stop this. It's taking hours. How I wish this had never
happened.

Chapter 5

Issues of Care

In reading this journal, I experienced in a very small way what Raymond was feeling. I wanted to stop from time to time in my reading of the journal and protest what I thought was a misrepresentation in his writing of my actions and statements. I caught a glimpse of and understood Raymond's despair, and I felt responsible for his pain. To borrow from Geertz (1988), as a result of Raymond's response, I found myself in a state of "moral hypochondria" and immediately began "extensive soul searching." I retraced and examined the process we had gone through, the decisions that had been made along the way, the consequences of those decisions, and how things might have happened differently.

I had written the final report based on the two teachers' stories, my classroom observations, the teachers' writings, and our discussions. This document held no surprises for James. He had read and commented on my fieldnotes along the way. We had discussed emerging themes and interpretations, and he had also read and commented on portions of the report as I completed it. All in all, he was comfortable with the portrait of his teaching self. Raymond was not.

Throughout the project Raymond had read the fieldnotes from classroom observations, and we had spent many hours discussing emerging themes and tentative interpretations. Eventually I offered Raymond an account of my understanding of what he did in the classroom and why he did it. It seemed to me, I suggested to Raymond, that the teacher as a dominant and controlling force in the classroom, albeit in a different guise, continued to be evident, even in his new model of collaborative response teaching. Then I invited him to comment on my interpretation.

I had been reading Schatzman and Strauss' (1973) book, *Field Research: Strategies for Natural Sociology*, in which the authors outline a technique they refer to as "Offering Interpretations or Testing Propositions." Since I had just offered my interpretation of his practice to Raymond, I was interested to read in Schatzman and Strauss (1973) that the response to such an offering can go one of two ways:

1. The researcher is told—one way or the other—that he simply does not understand, partially or completely. . . .
2. The researcher is told that his formulation is correct, or better still, that the informant "had never thought of it that way." Here the researcher gets a measure of validation, and makes something of a contribution to someone's understanding of himself. (pp. 81–82)

Raymond responded to my interpretation of his practice precisely as Schatzman and Strauss predicted. He replied, "Well—yes—I never thought about it that way. I'll have to think about that." The next time we met he turned our conversation immediately to this point and again confirmed my interpretation. He told me how much our conversations made him think and went on to explain to me how it was precisely his controlling presence that provided the classroom structure that allowed students to work in the way that he wanted them to work. To my mind, Raymond had given me the measure of validation or verisimilitude that Schatzman and Strauss (1973) spoke of, and this interpretation was thus incorporated into my report.

Raymond had declined to read drafts of each portion of the report as I completed it, suggesting instead that I just tell him what I was writing and he would read it when the whole document was completed. I did as he asked and we talked about what I was writing. But clearly, at the end of the project, Raymond was not prepared for the overwhelming impact of all his stories and all of our conversations collected together and fixed before him in print. And I was not prepared for the pain and anguish he felt.

When he called me after he had read the report, he said, "It's true, but that's not how I want to see myself." Raymond had always been excited about being part of the research project, and despite my attempts at maintaining his anonymity and that of his school, he talked freely to people about the project he was involved in. Given the many accolades he had already received as an innovative teacher, I felt that he expected that I would produce an equally pleasing portrait of his teaching self. And when the portrayal was not at all what he had envisioned it to be, he was devastated. He spent the next three days pouring out his pain to me in his journal, spilling it out on page after page, angry with me because I hadn't observed certain classes which would have shown him in a different light; angry with me because I had not shared James' stories with him beforehand, because then, he, Raymond, could have shown me a different side of himself; and hurt because I had not portrayed him as the teacher he wanted to be.

Here was a man who had given freely and enthusiastically of his time, a man I had worked with for over two years, a man whom I respected and cared for as a fellow human being, and I felt directly responsible for the anguish he was suffering. We had discussed the central thesis of the report that I was writing. I had offered him my interpretations of his classroom practice. Had he not heard my words? Had he not wanted to hear? Had I not pursued the topic often enough? Had I not done enough to convey my understandings or interpretations to Raymond, knowing that these interpretations would be problematic?

The report and the research project as a whole raised a host of ethical issues. How would the manner in which we worked together withstand critical examination? The report created for Raymond an awareness of himself as a teacher that, once expressed, could not be erased. Having created this awareness, what were my responsibilities toward Raymond? How well informed had Raymond been at the outset of our research project? Could we have anticipated this outcome, and would he have consented to take part in the inquiry if he had known where our questions would lead us? How had my questions or, for that matter, my silences helped to shape Raymond's stories? How had I received these stories? And once Raymond gave me his stories, were they mine?

This chapter will not necessarily offer solutions to all the ethical issues that arose from my work with Raymond, and certainly this chapter will not provide solutions satisfactory to all who read it. Instead, I hope that my reflections will open up and raise for discussion a number of issues associated with the study of teaching and teacher development.

Noddings' (1984, 1987, 1991, 1992) ethic of caring and her notions of fidelity gave me an alternative perspective from which to re-view my work with Raymond. Her writings provided me with another framework within which to situate the issues that arose from my research.

THE ETHIC OF CARING

Relationship lies at the heart of Noddings' ethic of caring. The relatedness that is so fundamental to our being induces caring. Natural caring, explains Noddings (1987), "establishes the ideal for ethical caring, and ethical caring initiates this ideal in its efforts to institute, maintain, or reestablish natural caring" (p. 385). How we relate to family and friends should therefore become our model for a caring relationship, and a primary fidelity to persons should guide our thinking during research. Noddings emphasizes the importance of genuine mutuality, truly collaborative inquiry, and research practices informed by a caring attitude toward others. She argues that the quality and depth of research on teaching would be enhanced if the virtue of fidelity were placed at the center of this work. She defines fidelity not as faithfulness to duty or principle, but rather as faithfulness attached to those with whom we are in relation. Noddings writes that an ethic of caring takes fidelity to persons as primary, and when faced with a research decision, she suggests that we make our decision on the basis of answers to these questions: "What effect will [this decision] have on the present relation? What effect will it have on the development of this person as a caring person? What effect will it have on our community of caring?" (Noddings, 1987, p. 390).

Research on teaching that is grounded in an ethic of caring would not make teachers the objects of research. Instead, Noddings suggests that problems that are of interest to both teachers and researchers should be chosen as the object of research. When both parties are meaningfully involved in the same problem or the same inquiry, the relationship between researcher and researched is fundamentally changed. Then the process of inquiry can become truly collaborative.

Noddings (1987) maintains that collaborative inquiry into issues of mutual interest, conducted in an atmosphere of trust and respect, would be more meaningful "research *for* teaching instead of simply research *on* teaching" (p. 394).

Within a collaborative inquiry relationship the traditional role of researcher as expert knower disappears, and there is no place in such a relationship for the researcher as objective, distant, or detached observer. Instead, the researcher becomes an engaged, involved coparticipant in the community of study. Because collaboration requires both a shared affinity and an interdependence, the lines separating researcher and researched blur. The hierarchical distinctions dissolve and the relationship moves toward a partnership of equals. The breakdown of the traditional compartmentalization of researcher and researched is both dependent upon and encourages the development of trust and dialogue characterized by openness. It is also the greater level of trust and caring between research partners that allows dialogue to develop into the deeper kind of conversational sharing that so richly informs the texts of narrative inquiry.

Does Caring Mean Concurring?

If much of the power and persuasiveness of collaborative narrative inquiry can be traced to the close long-term and trusting relationship between research partners, it is also this closeness that raises some of the most difficult ethical issues. Noddings offers guidance here, too. She acknowledges the value of rules of behavior to meet dilemmas encountered within a relationship, but the complexity and diffuseness of the ethical dimensions within any project of collaborative inquiry argue against pat formulas and simple solutions. Rules cannot guide us infallibly. Instead, each situation invites analysis on an individual basis. Noddings suggests that rules should be held loosely and tentatively, for consideration. But we must know also when to discard rules in order to deal in caring ways with the needs of others with whom we are in relation. Noddings (1984) portrays the person whose actions and decisions are rooted in caring and a regard for others in this way:

> Is the one-caring, then, a capricious and unprincipled character who is swayed this way and that by intensity, proximity, and the conditions of the moment? . . . Moral life based on caring is coherent, although it may defy description in terms of systematic consistency. It is swayed, but not determined, by intensity, proximity, and temporal conditions. The one-caring is dependable, not capricious. Her principles are guides to behavior, and she sees clearly that their function is largely to simplify situations, to prevent hundreds of similar questions from arising. She sees, also, that they may be of little use if a serious question actually arises. (p. 56)

Anticipating the dilemmas of researchers torn between fidelity to persons and fidelity to the research, to a funding body, or to an institution, Noddings posits the following case. After having worked with a teacher only to find that he or she is either incompetent, sexist, or racist, how should we respond? Can we address our concerns about this teacher's practice and still remain faithful to the teacher as a person, as well as to the trusting relationship we have built together? Noddings reminds us that the principle of fidelity or faithfulness to persons must remain inviolate, but that the problem of the teacher's incompetence, sexism, or racism must also be dealt with, and that it can be dealt with in a manner compatible with the tenets of an ethic of caring. Noddings eschews writing a negative report about a teacher's classroom practice. As Clandinin and Connelly (1988) explain, ''The research intention is to reconstruct the meaning in acts of schooling from the point of view of the actor rather than to judge the act from an external point of view'' (p. 271). A negative judgment or an unfavorable report is always hurtful, and when the judgment or the report comes from a trusted colleague it is doubly hurtful. There is a sense of betrayal because the interests of the research seem to have taken precedence over the importance of the relationship. While a Kantian interpretation of ethics would make it the researcher's duty to tell the "truth," and a utilitarian interpretation of ethics would seek a maximization of the greater good, the ethic of caring directs us differently. We are asked to consider what effect our actions will have on the relationship, on the development of the other as a caring person, and on our community of caring. We are asked to deal with the issues by affording our research partner "special treatment," much as we would offer it to each of our friends, and as we would wish it to be offered to us. Noddings (1987) uses the term "confirmation" to describe this aspect of a caring relationship. She writes, "As we work, talk, and debate together, we begin to perceive the ethical ideals that each of us strives toward. Then we are in a position to confirm—to help the other to actualize the best image" (p. 393). Confirmation asks that we attribute to the other the best possible motives, take into consideration what the teacher is trying to achieve, and, as with a friend, support the teacher's best qualities. Instead of writing a negative report about the teacher's practice, Noddings recommends that teacher and researcher enter into genuine dialogue, examining the issue together by checking interpretations and exploring meanings. In short, Noddings recommends talk. Talk as friends would.

Just as the research relationship is developed through conversation, problems within the relationship are also attended to through conversation. Van Manen (1977), in his definition of conversation, draws our attention to its relational quality, which underscores again the central element of Noddings' ethic of caring. He writes that conversation "is a type of dialogue which is not adversative but, as Socrates expressed it, 'like friends talking together'" (p. 218). In the practical working out of an ethic of caring, conversation and relationship are critically linked. Just as friends turn to conversation as a way of dealing with problems and coming to understand each other, conversation is also the characteristic method of research that seeks to understand people's understandings.

TRULY COLLABORATIVE INQUIRY

Raymond did not feel confirmed by the report as I had constructed it. Although not all readers of the report read his story as a negative one, Raymond did. For him, the report was hurtful. Initially, the aim of our project had been to examine good teaching practices in secondary school English classrooms. James' and Raymond's questions and our conversations together led us into tentative exploration of various aspects of their practices until suddenly, almost surprisingly, we found ourselves facing a direction that I had not envisioned at the start of the project. Although I had initiated the research relationship, it was at Raymond's urging that we changed direction and began to focus on the way in which the teachers' pasts functioned as a prelude to their present teaching practice. Raymond spoke often of how he had completely changed his approach in the classroom as well as in his personal life, and that there were aspects of his personal history that he felt were of great significance to the person he was and the teacher he had become. These conversations and hints at untold stories piqued my interest. When Raymond suggested to me that we needed to explore these changes and how they had happened, I agreed. I was excited about the new direction our research was taking, and so we sat down to renegotiate the terms of the original project. It was at this point that I asked if James and Raymond would be willing to commit more time to the project. I asked if I could be in their classrooms for the remainder of the school year, and if I might use the data collected for my doctoral dissertation. Both agreed, and we began.

Punch (1994), writing in the *Handbook of Qualitative Research*, advises researchers to spend some time thinking about the research they are becoming involved in, to reflect in advance on the ethical dilemmas they might face, and then just to go out and do the research. He favors this approach over one in which the researcher feels compelled to work within the guidelines of one research model only, lest this model prove to be inadequate or restrictive in the exploration of the complexities of the situation being studied.

So, with some background in the form of courses in qualitative research methods and a few preliminary studies as preparation, I went out and did the research. I entered the field as an educator with years of experience as a teacher, both at the high school and university level. I had a genuine interest in James' and Raymond's work as English teachers because I, too, had taught high school English for a number of years. I had also been away from the classroom for a number of years, and looked forward to learning from Raymond and James about their teaching practices, about what was new in the field and how things were being done differently. Not being a very experienced researcher, I did not identify with the traditional, hierarchial view of the researcher as the expert in the research relationship. Since both Raymond and James had more high school teaching experience than I did, I certainly did not feel like the expert as an observer-participant in their classrooms either. Rather, I hoped to learn from them as I completed the data-gathering for my dissertation.

Although I had not clearly articulated my own thinking about the researcher/researched relationships that I wanted to establish, honesty, integrity, confidentiality, and respect for persons were important to me. I brought these values as well as a desire for a collaborative working relationship to the project. My reading of Butt, Eisner, Grumet, Peshkin (1985), Pinar (1988), and especially the writings of Clandinin and Connelly then helped to shape for me a sense of the kind of research I wanted to do.

Clandinin and Connelly describe their work as narrative inquiry and define the research relationship within such inquiry as one in which the practitioner is a full partner in the research endeavor. In collaborative narrative inquiry, the university researcher and the teacher researcher are engaged in a mutual exploration of their own and each other's practices, and find themselves "in a relationship in which both practitioners and researchers feel cared for and have a voice with which to tell their stories" (Connelly & Clandinin, 1990, p. 4). The work of Connelly and Clandinin is based on the collection of classroom data and their biographical underpinnings, those personal, historical, and professional experiences that influence the routines, patterns, and habits of teachers. Biographical material is collected as explanatory material, recovered as various narrative unities are traced, so that the teachers' stories can be told with new meaning. Connelly and Clandinin (1990) contend that "Life's narratives are the context for making meaning of school situations" (p. 3). From a narrative perspective, "A school at any point in time is viewed as a story in which inquiry focuses on the developing text in a way that present and future are seen in terms of experiential reconstruction of the past" (Connelly & Clandinin, 1988, p. 109). Narrative inquiry proceeds over time, and a wide range of data is collected through methods of participant observation, interviews, and document analysis. These data are then arranged in such a way that an account of practice is given in the form of a narrative. The point of the narrative is an understanding of the persons being studied from the perspective of their own situation, rather than judgmentally from afar. The purpose is reconstruction of meaning rather than judgment of practice.

Teachers and researchers involved in narrative inquiry describe their work, explain their actions, express their thoughts, and recount educationally significant events drawn from their past. The structure of the story they tell, its narrative line, gives form to their ideas and meanings. Shaping stories is an activity that orders meaning, and in this way, narrative discourse contributes to knowing.

Although common sense would dictate that teachers occupy a central and active position within any inquiry into classroom practice, this has traditionally not been the case. Traditionally, teachers have played a more passive role, conditioned by their own training to allow researchers to explain events and make meaning of classroom actions. The kind of collaborative research practices that Connelly and Clandinin advocate and that Noddings' work suggests have only recently gained prominence. Philip Jackson's (1968) *Life in Classrooms* and the work of Lawrence Stenhouse (1967) are often cited as the beginning of a movement that has, especially within the last two decades, dramatically changed the way we think about and do classroom research. Cole and Knowles (1993), offering a brief overview of traditional and contemporary approaches to research, state that traditional "approaches to research on teacher development, based on assumptions reflecting an objective, logical deductive view of knowledge and a conception of teaching as a rational set of predictable behaviors essentially devoid of person and context increasingly are being passed over in favor of alternative approaches" (p. 475). They continue with the assertion that "Traditional approaches to educational research, broadly characterized as ahistorical, acontextual and apersonal, have been pushed aside to make room for alternative approaches in which the intensity of human actions and their meanings are centrally located" (p. 477).

The distinguishing feature of these alternative models of inquiry into teacher practice is the redefined relationship between the researcher and the researched. Cole and Knowles (1993) identify four phases within the research process and compare relationships and responsibilities of the researchers and the researched throughout these phases, in both traditional and more contemporary collaborative research practices. In traditional research models, the researcher has primary or sole responsibility in all four phases of the research activity: 1) planning and preparation, 2) information gathering, 3) interpretation and representation, and 4) reporting and use. The teacher plays a more passive role, consenting to the planning and preparation of the research activity, having some involvement in the data collection process, but usually having no involvement in the last two phases. By contrast, within partnership research as Cole and Knowles (1993) define it, the role of the teacher and the relationship between teacher and researcher changes dramatically. The matrix in Table 5.1 illustrates this change.

In reviewing the roles that Raymond and I played during the four phases of our research project, it becomes clear that our relationship did not always meet the requirements of partnership research as Cole and Knowles (1993) define them. Neither could our relationship be described as genuinely collaborative in the way that Connelly and Clandinin use the term. We did work together as partners in the planning

TABLE 5.1: Matrix for Considering Relationships and Responsibilities in Teacher Development Partnership Research

Phases of Research Activity

	PLANNING AND PREPARATION *(purpose, procedure, access, roles, logistics of time and place)*	**INFORMATION GATHERING** *(participation, observation, interviews, taping, written accounts)*	**INTERPRETATION AND REPRESENTATION** *(verification, validation, voice)*	**REPORTING AND USE** *(voice, control, benefits, public/ private use)*
TEACHER *(person affiliated with report and an institution primarily oriented toward practice)*	Negotiated participation in terms of perceived benefit, commitment, and procedure	Identification of information sources and negotiation of appropriate strategies	Responsive to preliminary analyses; mutual interpretation leading to final analysis	Negotiated representation in report and editing of personal accounts; perceived mutual benefit
RESEARCHER *(person affiliated with a research institution)*	Primary responsibility for articulation of purpose, coordination of research, and negotiation of activities	Identification of possible strategies and primary responsibility for gathering mutually agreed upon information	Preparation and presentation of preliminary analysis; mutual interpretation of preliminary analysis leading to final analysis	Primary responsibility for writing account; responsive to teachers' editorial and representational comments, perceived mutual benefit

Source: (Cole & Knowles, 1993, p. 480). Copyright © 1993 by the American Educational Research Association. Reprinted by permission of the publisher.

and preparation stage. I made the initial contact with Raymond and introduced the possibility of a research project. Raymond responded with enthusiasm and immediately offered to look after some of the entry procedures. He ensured that I would be allowed access to his classroom by clearing the way with the school's administration. Then we negotiated the logistics of time and place. We agreed that I would come on those days when he was scheduled to teach the most, so that I could be part of as many classes as possible, and see as much of a cross-section of his students as possible. Raymond also generously offered his time before and after classes so that we could talk about the day's happenings. We discussed the mutual benefits of my being there. I felt that I would learn about secondary school English practices by being in this experienced teacher's class, be able to do the research for my doctoral dissertation, and possibly also be able to make a contribution to the research on teacher practice. Raymond saw it as an opportunity to explore his own practice and to talk to someone about his teaching, an opportunity rarely afforded to him or most other teachers. He thought that through my questions he might gain new insights into his own practice. He also felt strongly about giving something back to the teaching profession and felt that our work together would inform classroom practice at a level beyond just his school.

We also worked as partners in the second, or "information gathering," phase. Together we planned how we would collect our data. Raymond encouraged taping our conversations, and occasionally we did. He suggested that we videotape the classes, and he opened his files to me, inviting me to read whatever materials interested me. Whenever he felt that either my pace or my questioning focus needed adjusting, he urged me to, as he put it, "probe more deeply" or "move more quickly." He collected his own published and unpublished writings, suggesting that these might offer additional insights beyond those gained through observations in his classroom and our many conversations. I made the fieldnotes throughout our work together, and Raymond received these at regular intervals. I had expected that his responses to the fieldnotes would fuel our ongoing conversations, but he commented very little, making only occasional corrections in the margins of my notes or adding explanations for events that I had not grasped completely.

Early on in the project, I attached the following suggestions to a set of fieldnotes before I gave them to Raymond:

Feel free to comment on:

>   Things in my notes that interest you
>   Anything remarkable or mystifying

What you were/are thinking at any particular point
Anything you would like to elaborate on and explain, or correct
Your comments will ensure that I don't misrepresent anything.

The fieldnotes to which this request was attached covered class-room events and conversations for the period from November 8 to December 13, 1989. Raymond made only one notation in this set of fieldnotes, providing further explanation for an incident that occurred on November 13, 1989, and that I had noted as follows:

Class over a little early. He [Raymond] said no one to open door till he said so. Girl defied him. T. [Teacher] called her back. Wanted her to stay behind after others left. She refused. He let her go.

Raymond's explanatory comments, as he wrote them in the margin of my fieldnotes, follow:

One week later she requests penalty time after 3:30 to make up for leaving and for minutes lost going to the washroom.
Serves 14 minutes.
Note: Also sort of a joke. She loves to defy males. Teacher is one, therefore teacher must also give her some room.

Attached to another set of fieldnotes when he returned them to me was this note:

January 29, 1990
Comment:
Frightening to realize teacher language abuse during extemporaneous talk. Also of note that too often, good ideas are not followed through during succeeding days, e.g. p. 13 last part of page.
Don't you find this tedious?

This was the total response to fieldnotes covering five weeks of classroom activity, and the brevity of this response is representative of the amount that Raymond wrote each time. We discussed the three points he raised in his January 29, 1990, notes and I assured Raymond first of all that I didn't find the data gathering and recording tedious. Using a funnel metaphor, I compared the vast amount of information that I was recording now at the beginning of our study to the large mouth of a funnel. And just as the funnel narrows, I explained, in time we too would narrow down our areas of focus and data collection.

We also talked briefly about the problem that Raymond identified of not following through on good ideas, and then exchanged some stories and examples from our practice. Raymond's surprise at his own use of language as it is recorded in the fieldnotes is similar to the experience Schroeder (Brody, Schroeder, Webb, Schulz, & Richert, 1994) describes in her work with teachers. But while Schroeder and the teachers in her study made their concern about what Raymond described as "language abuse during extemporaneous talk" a central issue of their project, we did not. I did not perceive the representation of language as a major issue for Raymond. We merely talked about the fact that the spoken word is usually not as carefully uttered as the written word is chosen, and compared the experience of seeing our spoken words in print to the experience of hearing our voices on tape. The first few times that we hear our taped voice we recognize that it is our voice, but at the same time, we cannot believe that we sound like that. In retrospect, of course, this conversation about the shock of seeing oneself represented in print anticipates Raymond's response to the final report. It also points to the larger issue, dealt with later on in this chapter, of how we as researchers receive and respond to teachers' stories.

Instead of detailed responses to the fieldnotes that I had made, Raymond offered me his journal writings. These were stream-of-consciousness entries prompted at times by the fieldnotes, but more often the entries were prompted by thoughts that had developed during his daily run. These journals then became the subject of many of our conversations, in which both of us put forth our interpretations and preliminary analyses. Mutually, we drew together many of the threads of Raymond's past, and saw how these had become interwoven into his present practice. Raymond was actively involved in this third phase, which Cole and Knowles (1993) refer to as "interpretation and representation." But his involvement was less than completely satisfying because I undertook the responsibility for the final analysis and the written report. In the fourth, "reporting and use" phase, the traditional compartmentalization of researcher and researched appeared. As researcher, I assumed interpretive authority and authored the final report.

From the perspective of collaborative narrative inquiry, this final report should have been co-authored. A co-authored report would have reflected our ongoing conversations and negotiations of what counted for truth and how our truths were to be represented. Discussions and collaborative writing should have been ongoing throughout the study, but even at this point, when Raymond resisted the way in which I had portrayed him, we could have undertaken steps to resolve the dilemma. As a first step, we might have recategorized the report as an interim rather than a final report. Then, as Noddings suggests friends would do, we could have discussed the issues in the report that were of concern to Raymond. We might have come to new understandings as we explored together the meanings of our words and the nuances within our interpretations. We could have begun the work of co-authoring a new document that was more confirming for Raymond, yet at the same time allowed both of our voices to be heard. In this way, the principle of fidelity would have been honored in the fourth and final stage of the research as well.

But at the time I questioned whether embarking on a new phase of examination and inquiry, followed by the process of collaboratively authoring a new report, was warranted. Raymond and I had worked together for over two years. I felt that I had conducted the study with integrity and that the data supported my conclusions. Certainly James, with whom I had worked in a parallel fashion, was comfortable with the way in which I had conducted the research, and with its outcome. Raymond acknowledged that he had read my preliminary notes, and pronounced my portrait of his teaching self as generally true, even though it was not as he wished to be portrayed. I felt that rewriting and changing the report at this point would have made us guilty of "narrative smoothing" (Connelly & Clandinin, 1990, p. 10), of reconstructing the narrative solely for the purpose of achieving an "all is well, happily-ever-after" ending. Therefore, I submitted the report as it was. But I continued to feel uneasy about the aftermath of our work together. Certainly Raymond did not feel confirmed by this report, and I felt that leaving the project at this point, without attending to the consequences, would have been a form of betrayal. Therefore, our working relationship did not end. Raymond and I continued to keep in touch while I spent a lot of time thinking about, reading about, and learning about how we might have done things differently.

Reading Geertz's (1973) work gave me some initial reassurance. In writing about the process of describing and interpreting events and experiences, Geertz reminds us that "Cultural analysis is intrinsically incomplete" (p. 29). What we can capture through our memory and convey through language is limited. It is but a sliver of the totality of any experience. Consequently, Geertz (1973) says of fieldwork in general that "to get somewhere with the matter at hand is to intensify the suspicion . . . that you are not quite getting it right" (p. 29). Wolcott (1990) illustrates this sense of getting it not quite right, yet not all wrong, with a research story that in many ways parallels Raymond's story. As part of an explanation of how he conducts his work and how he tries to satisfy the implicit challenge of validity (although he does not use this term in its original technical manner), Wolcott outlines his activities in the various stages of fieldwork and describes how these are intended not only to ensure the integrity of his work, but also "to convey ideas in such a way that the *reader*, who is also not quite getting it right, is not getting it wrong, either" (p. 133, emphasis in the original). Wolcott explains that he imposes what he refers to as a "rigorous subjectivity" on his writing drafts to satisfy himself that what he has rendered meets the demands of "elusive criteria like balance, fairness, completeness, sensitivity" (p. 133). Despite this, Wolcott reports that he has never conducted a study in which he has gotten it just right. To illustrate, he recounts his experience with Ed Bell, in a study of the principalship initiated in 1966. Wolcott reports that Bell reacted unfavorably to the way in which he had been portrayed in his role as a principal. Much as Raymond had, Bell also acknowledged the accuracy of Wolcott's reporting, but questioned whether it was a balanced report. Bell expressed dismay that Wolcott had devoted so much time and attention to chronicling the problems he faced as a principal. Twenty years after initiating the study, Wolcott, in conversation with Bell, discovered that Bell had forgotten the disappointment he had initially expressed at the perceived lack of balance in the report. Instead, Bell underscored the value of the study and how it had helped him "to see things that needed improving" (p. 134).

It remains to be seen whether, or how, Raymond's perception of our work together will change over time. I was more occupied with present concerns about how this report was affecting Raymond. I placed myself in his position. How might I respond if a researcher's portrait did not match my perception of myself? Smith (1990) describes just such a situation, encountered in his work in the Kensington School study. He had been asked to study a newly designed school building, as well as its newly designed program and organization. Smith reports that in this, his second field study, he tried for a kind of collegiality with the school staff. He reports that he was feeling his way along in the project, having no clear notion of what would later arise as ethical issues. Afterwards, in reflecting on the Kensington study in the book written as a result of it, Smith outlines a number of ethical issues, one of which closely parallels the issue Raymond and I were grappling with. Smith (1990) concludes that:

> One of the most difficult issues we live with from the original Kensington study is the knowledge that some of our portraits of people in the school

and the district did not match their own perceptions of themselves; they were less than pleased with the images we reflected back to them. These images of persons and practices seemed important for our story and seemed to be as well grounded in the data as we could make them. We had no special malice toward anyone; we did our best to see the world from their perspectives. Yet somehow, from their point of view, we had come up short. Even now I do not see any easy resolution to this dilemma. (pp. 265–266)

Raymond and I felt challenged to seek a resolution. Both James and Raymond had commented from time to time how much they appreciated being listened to, and having someone they could discuss their work with. But had they benefited in any other way from this research? Noddings (1987) suggests that we do not benefit as much from research that is conducted *on* teaching as we do from research that is conducted *for* teaching. Of what benefit was the research we had done? I had conveyed my understanding of Raymond's work in his classroom. We had not constructed a narrative of our understanding of our work together in the classroom. How might we have worked together differently?

Ours had not been the kind of genuinely collaborative relationship that Connelly and Clandinin (1988, 1990) advocate, and that Noddings (1984, 1987) describes as central to the ethic of caring. Nor was it the kind of partnership research that Cole and Knowles (1993) write about. Elements of collaboration were present, and certainly our relationship could be described as congenial, responsive, and caring. But primarily it was cooperative, rather than fully collaborative. If our relationship had been truly collaborative, I would not have been doing research on someone else. Instead, the teachers and I would have been inquiring into a problem or issue that was of mutual interest. As it was, the focus of our research was the teachers and their practice. Although the teachers, and especially Raymond, were instrumental in defining our research focus, the research was not a reciprocal endeavor. My stories were not under scrutiny, and my practices were not under inquiry. They remained in the background, functioning primarily in a support role, as story starters in our conversations. Although Raymond and I worked collaboratively in a number of aspects—establishing the focus of our research, identifying information sources, negotiating data-gathering procedures, and responding to preliminary interpretations—our collaboration was not sustained. We did not assume joint responsibility for the final analyses and report. Throughout, I had encouraged the teachers' voices and had participated in the conversations, but in the final stage I assumed the traditional privileged position of researcher as interpretive authority over the researched. Much as I felt Raymond had done in his teaching practice, I too had adopted only some of the elements of a new research approach. Although I was using the language of this new methodology, in many ways I continued to cling to the old ways even as I proclaimed the new.

By nature, partnered research is a reciprocal endeavor. In partnered research, it is important to decide the division of labor so that both persons feel they are contributing equally, if differently, throughout the inquiry. Although the interdependence of partners in collaborative research serves to dissolve the traditional compartmentalization of researched and researcher roles, the reality of the research site usually means that the classroom teacher has less time to devote to the project than the university participant does. In division of labor discussions, the question of who will write becomes central. Keeping journals, making fieldnotes, and co-authoring the final research text are very time-consuming activities. What is to be done if the teacher is not inclined to write, and it seems that the best thing for the relationship is for the university participant to be the primary recorder and interpreter? Whose knowledge is represented then?

In responding to these questions, Celeste Brody (Brody et al., 1994) invites us to think about the requirements of fidelity and care in collaborative narrative inquiry as evolving and changing as the collaboration and the relationship itself matures. She recounts her experience in a sixth-grade classroom where she co-taught with Marilyn over the course of one school year. Co-teaching seemed for Brody to be the only way she could conduct collaborative narrative inquiry consistent with her understanding of the ethic of care. She writes that it was an easy collaboration in terms of the co-teaching because both she and Marilyn valued relationships and their tending. But she also struggled with issues of unequal power, due mostly to the different roles and available time that the classroom teacher and university researcher had for learning and growing professionally. What was never very clear was how to navigate the remnants of traditional power relationships between university teacher and classroom teacher. Brody reports that Marilyn, like so many other teachers she had worked with, had in the past experienced a diminished sense of self when she was the object of university-level experts. Consequently, the two began co-teaching by emphasizing the "we" of the connection and exploring the dialectic of expert and learner.

In tracing the changing and evolving nature of the requirements of fidelity within a research relationship, Brody writes that fidelity begins with the researcher's commitment to the teacher, who must believe that the collaboration will benefit both her and her learning. In a co-teaching relationship, the primary questions are about how to share the same context, live in the same classroom, and see the situation through each other's eyes. Intimately connected to this is the commitment to acknowledging and respecting difference in the relationship.

Brody had hoped that Marilyn would keep a journal and read the fieldnotes in order to give her feedback, but much as Raymond had done, Marilyn preferred to respond orally. Brody was then compelled to experiment with ways that respected Marilyn's oral processing preference and her need for leisure time that did not include reading fieldnotes.

Fidelity begins with commitment to the teacher, but once both partners feel that there is sufficient trust and honesty between them, the cultivation of fidelity and care shifts to the process of co-reflection, where the co-teachers notice and name what they know and how they know together. Researcher and teacher work together to capture more completely the complexity, specificity, and interconnectedness of the classroom phenomena, while continuing to develop the relationship. The requirements of fidelity at this point are such that both partners take risks, exploring intentions and revealing values and beliefs.

The concern for fidelity and the care for the relationship shifts again when teacher and researcher are ready to take the lessons from the classroom to a larger public community through speaking and writing. Although she was willing to help in any way that she could, Marilyn did not want to share in the task of writing. The dictates of care in a relationship mean understanding the time limits of a busy teacher and negotiating the division of labor so that both persons feel that they are contributing equally but differently to the collaborative inquiry. As the author of the research text, Brody felt it was her responsibility to draw out Marilyn's meanings and represent them as accurately as she could. She experimented with new forms and structures to convey the different yet cohesive voices. She placed her voice followed by Marilyn's voice in the text, or she placed their transcribed dialogue in the text alongside their interpretations of its meaning. But the further she moved from the shared moment and the shared text, the more difficult it became for Brody to remain faithful to her partner's voice. Brody was the one revisiting the text and inventing the words. Marilyn would read it, validate, it or suggest changes, but it was no longer their text or their evolving meaning. Fidelity had shifted, then, from concern for the narrative of relationship to the public requirements of structure and form, and the integrity of the narrative itself.

Genuine Mutuality

Raymond very acutely felt the effects of not having been part of the final writing process. I felt that he regarded the completed research text as a "betrayal rather than a portrayal" (Clandinin, 1994). He felt the pain of visibility as Lightfoot (1983) describes it. He felt objectified by being studied and interpreted. He finds company for these feelings in Clandinin and Connelly's (1988) description of an ethical incident that occurred as part of a long-term collaborative research project they conducted in an elementary school. Ellen, a third-grade teacher, had asked if she could become involved with an already in-progress study, and cited reasons that in many ways were similar to those offered by Raymond. Ellen wrote, "I wanted to participate, hoping to be challenged and questioned about my practices—perhaps gain new insights, understandings which would affect my practice. I thought it would be an opportunity to engage in a meaningful discourse, I wanted another adult in the classroom with whom I could share this experience" (p. 274). A problem developed when Charles, the researcher, wrote an interpretive account of his work with Ellen and distributed it for discussion in a doctoral seminar that he was enrolled in. The distributed paper contained Charles' evaluative comments on Ellen's personal and professional actions. To compound matters, Charles had also used the teacher's real name and the names of students. Ellen was upset that names had been used in the paper, and offended that evaluative comments had been made without discussion. With regard to this latter point, Ellen felt that care and respect had not been shown, given the sensitivity of the information that Charles possessed. Further, she felt that Charles' treatment of her "was quite external and objective, and didn't seem to be looking at things from her point of view" (p. 275).

A number of other factors at play in this incident, including the fact that Charles' research interests were different from those of the larger project that he was a part of, prompted his eventual withdrawal from Ellen's classroom. In reviewing the ethical issues of this case, Clandinin and Connelly (1988) note that continual discussion did not mark Charles and Ellen's work together. A shared research purpose had not evolved in their relationship, since Ellen's purposes were not being served by Charles' presence in her classroom. Charles remained an observer in Ellen's classroom, offering interpretations of her personal practical knowledge, but never became a participant in the classroom as Ellen had anticipated he would. Clandinin and Connelly (1988) conclude their account of this incident by emphasizing the importance of relationship for successful collaborative research: "In everyday life, the idea of friendship implies a sharing, an interpenetration of two or more persons' spheres of experience. Mere contact is acquaintanceship, not friendship. The same may be said for collaborative research which requires a close relationship akin to friendship" (p. 281).

Martin Buber (1965) also writes of the importance of relationship and our responsibilities to persons with whom we are in relation. Although he addresses the teaching–learning relationship, his work is equally significant for thinking about the researcher–practitioner relationship. Buber's dialogue model of teaching stems from his belief that there are two basic modes of existence: I-Thou, and I-It. He tells us that the basic words that people speak are not single words, but word pairs. They are the word pairs I-Thou and I-It. The basic word pair I-Thou establishes relation. An I-Thou relationship is based on respect for the individual. It honors the personal. It acknowledges the importance of relationships, and the uniqueness of each person, situation, and experience encountered in the classroom. In an I-It relationship, the teacher brings the student into a relationship with an academic discipline. The teacher is an "It" whose function it is to relate the student to knowledge, and the student is the "It" to be initiated into this relationship. This pairing fails to relate either the student or teacher to the other as Thou. Buber calls on teachers to enter into an I-Thou relationship with their students. Living in an I-Thou relationship requires that student and teacher engage in dialogue, a dialogue characterized by the mutual sharing of experience. In Buber's view, trust and mutuality should be the central elements of the teaching relationship, and by extension, also the research relationship. Trust and mutuality can be achieved by entering into the life of the individual and unique person who is the other, by being in relation to another, and by standing with that person in the common situation of educating and being educated. This act of inclusion creates the mutuality and trust that make true dialogue possible. Buber also writes about the importance of confirmation and the need for confirmation to become a part of this dialogue:

> . . . to realize one's created uniqueness, one must be confirmed by others in his personal qualities and capacities, in his right and responsibility to become what only he can become. . . . (as cited in Scudder, 1971, p. 205)

Buber's emphasis on relationship, dialogue, and confirmation brings us back again to Noddings' ethic of caring and the notion of fidelity. Although an ethic of caring cannot provide specific solutions to our ethical dilemmas or give us specific rules to follow, it does provide us with a guiding framework in the form of questions we can ask and directions we can take in our work with teachers.

Caring Research Practices

The conversations that Raymond and I had during the time that we worked together gave shape to the final written report that was so painful for him. Using Noddings' notion of fidelity—of being faithful to persons and the expectations established in relation—as a guide, I would like to examine the nature of these rooted-in-conversation research practices that played such a large part in our study. How did my questions or my silences shape our conversations? How did I respond to Raymond's stories? How did I receive them? Research conducted in an atmosphere of mutual trust encourages the telling of personal stories. And while such research can yield rich, powerful, and very compelling data, collaboration can also lead to unexpected complications. How did we deal with the ethical tensions that arose in the small moments of our experience together? How might we have dealt with these tensions differently? How can we share the stories told within a research context and speak to their multiple meanings in caring, moral, and ethical ways?

Informed consent. Initially the purpose of our study was to examine good secondary school English teaching practices, and both James and Raymond consented to my presence in their classrooms. We began by exploring various aspects of their practice, but eventually our conversations led us to focus on the way in which the teachers' past functioned as a prologue to their present teaching practice. We discussed the new direction that our inquiry was taking, talked about how this new focus would become the basis for my doctoral dissertation, and worked out a time frame for my presence in their classrooms. I shared with James and Raymond as much as I knew about this new journey of inquiry we were embarking on, and again both teachers consented to continue on. But the stories that unfolded as we worked together were not what I could have predicted at the beginning of the project. And neither Raymond nor I anticipated the eventual outcome of the inquiry. Would he have consented to take part in the inquiry if he had known where our questions and our conversations would lead us?

In the traditional sense, the concept of informed consent means that the individuals involved in a study completely understand not only what is expected of them, but also the possible consequences of having taken part in the study. It is not possible when working with emergent themes to try to satisfy the demands for the kind of clear-cut statements of intent and consequence that are traditionally associated with informed consent. A more appropriate ethical guideline in narrative research is the concept of ongoing, continual negotiation in conversation, characterized by honesty and candor, and built on mutual trust and respect. As with friends, within a collaborative research relationship, participants enter into discussions with an open agenda, guided not by rules and standards or by proper signatures on a standardized consent form, but by the relationship at hand.

The significance of relationship for the research also alerts us to consider the ethical consequences of that relationship. Richert (Brody et al., 1994) cites change as one of the most compelling of these ethical issues. Although clear-cut statements of intent and consequence, as they have traditionally been defined, are not possible within a collaborative research framework, Richert suggests that change, however, is a predictable outcome of any research process. Both researcher and participant change in the course of their work together. Richert contends that in a relationship that occurs within the context of a research project where the purpose is to understand a phenomenon, the people working together on the inquiry will change as a result of their inquiry. They will come to know more, and to understand more about what they are studying. But these changes in their knowledge and understanding can also be negative. Participants might come face to face with ideas and understandings that are disquieting and that they would rather not encounter. Through the research they might be confronted with images of themselves that, like it or not, remain with them. Richert (Brody et al., 1994) suggests that "As people begin to examine what they do and why they do it—a natural outcome of the research relationship—new doors open whether or not they are invited to open." For this reason, it is important to examine the nature of the research relationship and the responsibility of the one who initiated the research to inform research colleagues, before they consent to enter into a research partnership, about the possibility of change occurring.

If we wish to do our research in a more mindful way, let us give thought to the responsibilities we have within the research relationship to begin conversations with our teacher colleagues about anticipated change. When our research practices are grounded in beliefs about the importance of relationship, fidelity, and caring, these beliefs guide our thinking and the ways in which we engage teachers in conversation.

Confidentiality. In research activities where identities are buried under numbers and within statistical formulae, guarantees of privacy, anonymity, and confidentiality are more easily met than within research activities characterized by face-to-face interactions. And issues of privacy and confidentiality loom even larger when descriptive studies are done closer to home and identities become more difficult to disguise. Traditionally, our response to these issues has been to provide pseudonyms for participants and to change place names. But as Lincoln (1990) reminds us, "It must be remembered that laws and regulations regarding confidentiality, privacy, and anonymity for research respondents were framed under epistemologies and ontologies (i.e., logical positivism and post-positivism) that are now believed to be *inadequate* and indeed, *misleading* for human inquiry" (p. 279).

As we move further and further away from paternalistic research paradigms, we begin to question more and more the need for the old rules governing confidentiality, privacy, and anonymity. When we begin to see research participants in a new way—no longer as subjects needing protection—then we also begin to rethink the rules that govern our relationship. The word *subject* can be traced to the Latin *sub jugere*, meaning to place under the yoke, or to enslave. When the term "subject" is no longer a part of our research language, then we can begin to view our research relationships with teachers differently. When we think of the teachers we work with as collaborators and full partners in the research endeavor, we enter into a new working relationship. And within the framework of this new professional relationship, our understanding of what constitutes ethical behavior also changes.

We might begin by examining the way in which we identify both the participants in our studies and the published authors from whose works we have drawn insights. Within the body of our research texts we traditionally refer to other authors and researchers by their surnames. For example, I attributed a quote cited at the beginning of this section, to Lincoln. I used neither the author's given name, Yvonna, nor her initials, Y.S., relying entirely on the surname to identify my source. When, however, we refer in the body of our research texts to teachers we have worked with, these teachers are generally given pseudonyms and referred to by their given names only. Readers of my research study, for example, are introduced to two high school English teachers, James and Raymond. This time-honored method of identification perpetuates the traditional hierarchical distinctions between researchers and teachers. Furthermore, while we go on to identify published authors and researchers in full in our reference list, this courtesy is not extended to the teachers from whom we have gained as much, if not more, insight as we have gleaned from those whose writing has been published. While we are careful to cite correctly in our references the names of university researchers and writers and others whose works we have used, we are equally careful to hide the names of the teachers we work with, to ensure confidentiality and to protect their identities. Power is both exercised and acknowledged in the naming or withholding of names in a bibliography. And teachers, unacknowledged in the references and referred to throughout the text by their given names only, become, as it were, half-objects.

But as the hierarchical relationships of traditional methods of research give way to more collaborative forms of inquiry, where the researcher is no longer seen as having interpretive authority over the persons studied, then it becomes a matter of ethics not to ensure anonymity, but rather to give full naming credit to the co-participants in a study.

Reciprocal self-disclosure. Conversation is a central and critical element of narrative inquiry, and the quality of the relationship between research partners and the trust within that relationship affects the quality of the information being shared in conversation. Within a research context in which we work with teachers over a long period of time and have many conversations, it is through sharing and storytelling in conversation that our relationship develops. In conversation with friends we tell a story, and they in turn share one, which brings us closer together. It's a process that builds relationships. Within a genuine relationship of mutuality, we spontaneously share personal ideas, experiences, thoughts, and feelings. This may involve a degree of risk-taking on our part, but it is also the way we reveal ourselves as individuals. Talking about details of our daily life sends a message of rapport and caring and is a way of getting to know others better as individuals. Self-disclosures serve the function of establishing intimacy, and act as a form of modeling whereby the research partner is encouraged to respond in a similar vein. By the way in which we engage in conversation and show interest in and share our thoughts, ideas, and understandings, we nourish a friendship. By opening ourselves up to others, we invite a conversational balance; we create a symmetry in our conversation and open the way for our partner in conversation to feel comfortable about disclosing more.

The nature of these disclosures need not be dramatic, extended, or deeply intimate. James, for instance, was feeling a lot of pressure to use cooperative learning groups in his teaching. When I said that I had reservations about the frequency and the manner in which cooperative learning was being used in high school English classes, James responded with his own strong criticism of the practice. Until we had this conversation about cooperative learning, he had felt very isolated in his stance on the issue. Either all of the other teachers were in total support of cooperative learning, or were unwilling to publicly question the popular practice. Because I had expressed my reservations, James felt more comfortable sharing his. He wanted to publish his views on cooperative learning in the regional journal for teachers, and so we continued to debate the topic. I was able to direct him to the research literature on cooperative learning, and also provided feedback on drafts of his writing. This common concern about cooperative learning, although for different reasons and to different degrees, became part of the developing trust in our relationship and part of the pattern of our reciprocal storytelling.

But the topic of cooperative learning didn't figure nearly as prominently in the conversations that Raymond and I had, despite the fact that he was an ardent spokesperson for the practice, and worked with other teachers to help them in their understanding of the group process. I offered my thoughts on cooperative learning, and Raymond responded with his. Thereafter, although Raymond spoke often of his group teaching method, we didn't discuss our differences or address the topic either as frequently or as frankly as James and I had done. Was it easier to pursue these discussions with James because the conversations served to build a bridge between us? Was it merely prudent, or was it unethical, to be less open with Raymond on a topic that might create a barrier between us? Is it ethical within a research relationship to tell stories or reveal things in order to elicit a reciprocal self-disclosure that will further the data gathering for our inquiry? Alternatively, is it ethical to remain silent about some things for fear that speaking out might shut down the conversation and thus jeopardize our data gathering? Is it acceptable at times to sacrifice the relationship for data?

The practice of ethical and moral compromises in research is common. Kimmel (1989) maintains that trade-offs are necessary in research and that by doing good research one always acts a little unethically. Further, he questions whether we can in fact do research entirely without deception. Punch (1994) also argues that in the interests of collecting meaningful data and ensuring the validity of participant response, '' . . . it may be unavoidable that there is a degree of impression management, manipulation, concealment, economy with the truth, and even deception'' (p. 95).

But deception and exploitation are diametrically opposed to research methods wherein the researched is viewed as a full partner in a collaborative enterprise. When our research is based on principles of collaboration, we can anticipate a reciprocal relationship with our research partner. We can expect a relationship in which we share stories, share risks, and share in the research design from beginning to end. We can expect to become partners in the generation of knowledge. Adopting such a position has implications for what counts as ethical in our practice. An ethic of caring would suggest that self-disclosure should be a natural part of the process of building a relationship, not a gambit. And because reciprocal self-disclosure promotes intimacy, we have a responsibility to maintain the climate of caring and confirming that encouraged this intimacy. When our research practices are informed by a caring attitude toward others, our decisions are based on what effect our actions will have on the relationship, on the development of the other as a caring person, and on our community of caring.

Responding to stories. Reciprocal self-disclosure is a way of building trust between teacher and researcher, a trust that encourages conversation and storytelling. Although storytelling is at the heart of human conduct, it is only recently that we have begun to associate storytelling with professional development or educational research. Prevailing conceptions of what constitutes professional knowledge have generally disregarded teachers' stories. In the past, teachers have seldom been offered occasions to share with each other and to make public through stories a deeper understanding of their work. Teachers have rarely made these occasions for themselves because they have not valued storytelling as a way of organizing their experiences and constructing their knowledge (Bruner, 1990; Polkinghorne, 1988). Teachers have also been shaped by their training to look outside themselves for pedagogical knowledge. Inviting teachers to tell their stories and providing a forum for the telling is a first step in redressing the personal, professional, and public neglect of a narrative way of knowing. However, inviting teachers to tell their stories also opens up for consideration how their stories, once told, are received. Issues of relationship, response, and vulnerability arise.

The importance of relationship and the issue of trust in a collaborative research relationship cannot be overstressed. Kathie Webb (Brody et al., 1994) relates the following story as an illustration of the development of trust. As Kathie's research relationship with Janet Blond, a junior high school teacher, developed, Kathie found it increasingly difficult to separate when they were being friends from when they were doing research. During the course of non-research-related telephone conversations with Janet, Kathie found herself wondering about the ethics of taking notes during the conversations. Much of what Janet had to say seemed relevant to the study, yet it seemed inappropriate to make notes. She would not make notes if she were conversing with family or friends. How could she do it when she was in conversation with Janet? Between friends, conversations develop spontaneously. Within a collaborative partnership, conversation flows naturally, encouraged by the equality of the relationship of those in conversation. Interviews conducted specifically for the purpose of research can resemble conversations, but they are different because the researcher attends each conversation with a critical consciousness. Genuine conversations cannot be conducted. We are involved in them, and they have a spirit of their own. When she spoke to Janet about her dilemma, Janet assured her that she expected notes to be taken. Nevertheless, Kathie still felt uneasy. Her discomfort stemmed from a concern for fidelity to the person. She felt that Janet trusted her, and she questioned whether it was a breach of trust to listen between the lines of their discussions and make notes on their casual telephone conversations. She questioned the ethics of exploiting a friendship that had developed in the research context and wondered where the boundaries of research and relationship began and ended.

It takes time to develop a relationship in research. When Raymond felt comfortable enough with me, he shared many personal and professional stories. In turn, I tried to be faithful in my rendering of his stories as I recorded them in my fieldnotes and wrote the final report. But when he encountered them on the page, Raymond's own words often seemed alien to him. In his response, written a few days after he first read the completed report, Raymond expressed his pain at seeing his words in print, with phrases such as "it hurt to see it quoted." The following excerpts from Raymond's response, cited in full in the previous chapter, further illustrate the surprise and disbelief he felt upon reading his own words:

> phrases like "he could be a good teacher only if he imposed [himself] on the learning." stung as did the incoherent sequencing of statements—from "imposed . . . on learning" . . . to . . . "uneasiness" . . . to "akin to artists." How could he be so incoherent? Was he really that way?
>
> And finally, when he speaks of an ideal classroom, "The classroom . . . filled with walls of different books where students would embark on a search for meaning with materials *I give them.*" Not only wordy, inaccurately expressed, but also arrogant and controlling. How could he have said that?

When I read these and other such passages of protest in Raymond's response, two lines from T. S. Eliot (1963) echoed through my mind:

"That is not what I meant at all./That is not it, at all." These lines from Eliot's *The Love Song of J. Alfred Prufrock* seemed to capture Raymond's reaction to the strangeness of his own words. Interwoven throughout the whole of Eliot's poem are the themes of risk, vulnerability, relationship, and response that were also so central to our research. There are many parallels between the situation Prufrock finds himself in and the situations we find ourselves in when involved in narrative inquiry. In collaborative narrative inquiry, the relationship between researchers and participants is dynamic and continually developing. Trust between researcher and participant is necessary before we can move beyond casual conversations and risk asking the more meaningful questions, or telling our more meaningful stories. Then, before we begin our stories, we are faced with decisions of how we should frame the stories so that we can properly convey to our listeners just what it is we mean. Stories can make their tellers vulnerable. And so we consider how our stories will be received, whether the essence of what we have said will be understood.

In Eliot's *The Love Song of J. Alfred Prufrock*, we encounter a timid Prufrock in a room full of people, where the " . . . women come and go/Talking of Michelangelo." It is in this setting that Prufrock is gathering the courage to ask an "overwhelming question." But he is afraid. He wonders how he should frame the question. He questions whether he has "the strength to force the moment to its crisis"; whether he dares to "disturb the universe" with his asking. And if he should risk it, he wonders which words would best convey his meaning. He agonizes and asks, "Then how should I begin/To spit out all the butt ends of my days and ways?" The poem is filled with images that manifest the conflict between Prufrock's desire to relate to others and his need to withdraw. At certain moments in the poem, Prufrock views other persons exclusively as objects, seeing only parts of bodies rather than whole persons: "I have known the arms already, known them all—/Arms that are braceleted and white and bare. . . . /Arms that lie along a table, or wrap about a shawl." When he assumes this stance, he is cool and detached. But as soon as he sheds some of his objectivity, begins to see the whole person, and moves closer in relationship to the other, he also begins to lose his equanimity. He becomes disconcerted, afraid to risk disclosure, and retreats to the security of commonplace conversation. He seeks refuge in social decorum, in "the taking of a toast and tea." This withdrawal into social conventions is his strategy for maintaining distance from the other. And he justifies this distancing by proclaiming that "It is impossible to say just what I mean." As the poem draws to a close, we realize that Prufrock will not ask the overwhelming question: "Oh, do not ask, 'What is it?'/Let us go and make our visit." He has let the moment of opportunity pass. Instead of asking the question, he reveals to us, as readers, his fear of how his question might have been received.

In Debra Schroeder's (Brody et al., 1994) collaborative storytelling and story-writing project, the issues of relationship, response, and vulnerability also came to the fore when the teachers she was working with reacted to their own words in print much as Raymond had. Schroeder recounts how, much to her surprise, the teachers were horrified to see their spoken words in print when she returned the typed transcripts of their conversations to them. The transcripts seemed cold and revealing. The teachers felt exposed and vulnerable. In the ensuing discussions, the conversation that had once flowed naturally suddenly became very guarded and stilted as the teachers tried to ensure that their thoughts were spoken in complete and grammatically correct sentences. In responding to this situation, Schroeder was guided by Grumet (1987), who writes that "if telling a story requires giving oneself away, then we are obligated to devise a method of receiving stories that mediates the space between the self that tells, the self that told, and the self that listens: a method that returns a story to the teller that is both hers and not hers, that contains herself in good company" (p. 323).

Trying to situate the issue of receiving stories within Noddings' ethic of caring, Schroeder began to construct a framework for the "good company" that she hoped she and the teachers could be for each other in their research group. During the course of the research, the group probed the nature of their responses and explored the issue of vulnerability in their research relationships, in their willingness to participate, in the stories that were told, and ultimately in the knowledge they were able to construct. As the teachers became aware of Schroeder's own feelings of vulnerability and her concern over their discomfort, their vulnerability to the unforgiving transcripts lessened, and conversation returned to normal. A decision was made to rewrite the stories that would appear in the final research report in such a way that they would return the speaker's words to her in the good company of acceptable written language. Dismissing long-held notions of a single, fixed truth, Schroeder and the teachers decided that the words that were transcribed were not unalterable. In fact, often the transcripts had not captured the shades and deeper meanings that by way of tone originally infused the teachers' spoken words. Therefore, the group began to view the transcripts as just another part of their ongoing and ever-changing construction and reconstruction of meaning through storytelling. With this anecdote from her research experience, Schroeder helps us to think about our preoccupation with quotations and accurate citations, stripped bare of context, as fidelity to data. When our research practices are grounded in beliefs about the importance of relationship and fidelity to persons, the way in which we respond to the data of stories is changed. Schroeder (Brody et al., 1994) suggests that "if we redefined response not only as an answer but a promise to return something that has been entrusted to us in faith as a condition of our relationship to the teller, we would reposition ourselves ethically within the research relationship." Then we would begin to place as much importance on receiving and responding to stories in narrative research as we do on telling them. Then, I believe, we would be less likely to hear the protest "That is not what I meant at all./That is not it, at all." Instead, we might come closer to hearing a description such as this, found on the closing pages of Toni Morrison's *Beloved* (1987): "She is a friend of mine. She gather me. . . . The pieces I am, she gather them and give them back to me in all the right order. It's good, you know, when you got a woman who is a friend of your mind" (pp. 272–273).

COLLOQUY

It is difficult to predict the moral and ethical quandaries that we might wander into in our research. It is also difficult to know which small decisions will lead to larger dilemmas. Each research setting is bound to give rise to slightly different ethical issues. Although we have a responsibility to attempt to anticipate ethical problems and to conduct ourselves with integrity in the face of problems, we cannot possibly articulate in advance all the ethical dilemmas that might emerge during a study. Neither can we rely on rules and regulations to solve dilemmas arising unexpectedly out of the complex interactions of human relationships. It is the values that undergird our research methods and behaviors toward research participants that can guide us through the complexities of a situation. The ethical guidelines we follow in our personal lives as we deal in caring ways with family and friends can also guide us in our professional work. The ethic of caring, as Noddings (1987) suggests, can become an anchor to throw out whenever we find ourselves in danger of drifting away from persons, relations, and the principles of collaboration in our research work.

However, even as we pursue caring, collaborative research relationships, there continue to be attendant questions that face us and our co-researchers. Collaboration requires time, and while university researchers are given time for research as a part of their workload, schools do not include research as part of the teacher's job description. There-fore, teachers involved in research projects do this as something extra, receiving permission, but usually no other administrative support or encouragement. There is also a disparity in the reward structure for engaging in and publishing research. Both the university-based re-searcher and the teacher researcher may feel that they have benefited because they have been part of an exciting process of discovery and learning. In addition, the university researcher receives a number of tangible benefits: either a completed Ph.D., a reduced teaching load, merit pay, eventual tenure, and/or promotion. The teacher researchers can speak of the rewards of being listened to, of having meaningful conversations, and of sharing their work and thoughts with others. But they receive no salary or work benefits. We can speak of this disparity in benefits as an issue of status and power. It is difficult to tease out all of the discrete elements of the power dimensions within a research relationship, and this constitutes but one example. The power differen-tials between teachers and professors have developed over time, and have been shaped and strengthened by the story of time. These power relationships, where teachers have generally been considered subordi-nate to university professors, are not easily dissolved. Working in a collaborative relationship and co-authoring the research narrative is one way in which we can equalize this historical imbalance of power. But the tangible benefits do not reach such a state of equilibrium. They tend to accrue for one partner only. When faced with the long time-span needed to complete a research study in which both partners have shared the research roles, are we comfortable with the disparity of the conse-quent benefits? Can we say that each partner has benefited, only differ-ently?

At another level, we can also ask questions about the narrative research texts we write. I believe that Raymond's story offers some insights into teaching, the consistency of teaching practices, and the way in which this consistency is connected to a teacher's past. How is my writing of Raymond's story different from what it might have been if we had co-authored the story? What aspects did I fail to include in my rendering? What other aspects might we have captured if we had co-authored the narrative? How many facets are there to Raymond's story? To any one story? How many ways can it be told? And how many ways can it be read? It is these last questions that I wish to turn to in the following chapter.

Chapter 6

Narrative Meaning:
The Reader's Voice

Initially Raymond and I felt challenged to examine, and if possible to resolve, the dilemma of a research portrait that was less than pleasing to him. We met, we talked, and Raymond wholeheartedly supported the writing of a book as a way of bringing the issues we faced to the attention of a broader readership. What we had learned might be helpful to others. We agreed that as part of the co-authorship of the book, he would write another personal response journal, while I would inquire into the theoretical and academic questions of our research methodology. My inquiry led me to a reading of Noddings' work. When I introduced Raymond to the ethic of caring and the notion of fidelity as an alternative framework within which to structure the study of teaching, he responded immediately to the confirming possibilities of this approach. He read chapter drafts as I completed them and ''liked the direction'' I was taking in my writing.

His own writing was going to follow a rereading of the original study. Two years had passed since his first reading and his initial journal response to my written portrayal of him as a teacher. Another, perhaps more dispassionate, reading after the passage of some time might generate new understandings and a different response. But when he turned to this task, he found it difficult. He wrote a few pages very similar in tone to his first journal response, and realized that he still could not ''think even minimally objectively'' about the report. Consequently, our writing arrangement returned much to what it had been when we first started working together: I wrote, and occasionally Raymond and I met to discuss the work. Eventually Raymond decided to withdraw from the project entirely, citing several reasons. He was very busy and did not have time for writing or our discussions. He also felt that much had changed for him since the report was originally written. He had changed as a person and as a professional, so the first few chapters of the book did not portray him as he was now. He acknowledged that I had been ''right on'' in many instances, but that was then, and this is now. He was not the same teacher or person now that he had been five years earlier, when I last visited his classroom.

Using Lightfoot's (1983) terms, I had initially described Raymond's anguish at seeing himself as the pain of visibility. However, Raymond did not feel that he had been made visible to a reading audience. He did not feel that I had captured the full context of the classroom situation within which he worked, or all the facets of his voice and being. The closure of any study is a rhetorical device that seems to complete its story. Raymond was not happy with this completion, saying the study was only a partial representation. Because of the partiality of the portrayal and the added fact that he felt he was now no longer the person he had been then, he did not wish to be named as co-author. He asked, instead, that his anonymity continue to be ensured.

We spoke thereafter of the difficulty of actualizing the ideals of collaborative research. Raymond's concern that I had not represented all the dimensions of his teaching person and practice seemed to imply that a summation of all possible perspectives on his teaching could be achieved. This would not, however, account for our implicit knowledge that each perspective leaves a remainder that generates new visions, that there are an infinite number of possible perspectives from which to view any phenomenon. A process of collaboratively negotiated selection and reconstruction of events would have been more confirming for Raymond. Nevertheless, every configuration of his practice, once released to readers, would still become subject to the interpretive strategies of those readers, and the unique images of Raymond that their personal readings generated.

Despite his unhappiness with the teaching portrait he faced, Raymond did not think that he would have consented to write collaboratively even if he were able to replay the course of events in our research. Writing takes time and he did not have the time then, just as he does not feel he has the time now. He fully expected me to continue with my writing and to complete the book, even though he no longer wished to participate in the project.

James had said long ago that he was not interested in becoming a writing partner for the book. From his perspective, there was nothing more to reflect on. He had no objection to the idea of a book, but he had neither the time nor the inclination to participate in the writing of one. We did, however, sit down together to review the completed manuscript. James had only found time to read the chapter that contained his story, so our conversation centered there. At this point, six years after we had first started working together, James hardly recognized himself as he read through Chapter 2 again. ''Did I really have that much energy then?'' he asked. He, too, commented on how things had changed in the five years since I had last visited his classroom. He felt he didn't ''rail as much anymore about the new curriculum,'' because, as he said, ''You feel less certain about things as you get older.''

Raymond felt that I had represented him negatively and that James had been presented as the positive standard against which he, Raymond, was being evaluated. Others read the narratives differently. One reader saw both teachers as very controlling. She felt that James exercised his control through his teacher-centered approach, and felt that his inability to accommodate cooperative learning groups might be due to his unwillingness to share authority with students. She also questioned whether James cared about his students; she wondered what it was he did care for—being in control, perhaps?

Another reader felt intuitively drawn to Raymond as a teacher, seeing his approach as much more effective than James', especially for inner-city classrooms. Of even greater value to this reader was what she learned about herself by reading about James and Raymond. For her, their stories were one step removed from the pain of seeing herself as a practitioner, but they also brought her one step closer to understanding herself and her practice, and seeing the two more closely.

How many ways can we read James' and Raymond's stories? How do we find meaning in them? How do we read research narratives when they become textually embodied? What is the reader–text relationship? How do we, and in what ways, as readers, collaborate with texts to make meaning? Just as we assume different stances to read the classroom as text, either from an objective outsider's perspective or from a collaborative perspective of joint involvement, we can also assume different stances as we read the texts of narrative inquiry. Educational research has been influenced by numerous disciplines and has drawn on a variety of methods to produce its body of knowledge. The differing traditions of teaching research come out of disciplines as diverse as psychology, sociology, linguistics, anthropology, and philosophy. Drawing literary theory and the contributions of reading research into this nexus broadens our understanding of our experiences in education and contributes especially to our understanding of the texts of narrative inquiry.

For writing to be considered a narrative, a storyteller and a story are required. Traditionally we have distinguished between so-called ''real'' and literary narratives. We have held that while imaginative writing is false, truth can be found in reports, in scientific or otherwise transactional writing. This distinction is something we have known since childhood. The ominous tone in the parental question, ''Is that the truth, or are you making up a story?'' confirmed for us very early on that to avoid punishment it was truth, not a story, that we should tell. Although Heath (1983) clearly points out cultural settings where this is not the case—where story is valorized—it is not generally so in our academic communities. We hold different beliefs about which kind of narrative conveys truth. But these beliefs are open to question when we begin to recognize the narrative strategies we employ to construct all our narratives. On the pages of qualitative research studies we meet people who exist, and the stories recounted have happened. In literary narratives, the authors draw on their knowledge of real flesh-and-blood figures of everyday life to create their fictional characters. But as Geertz (1973) notes, ''The importance does not lie in the fact that [one] story was created while [the other] was only noted. The condition of their creation, and the point of it (to say nothing of the manner and quality) differ. But the one is as much a fictiō—'a making'—as the other'' (p. 16). Both are fictions in the sense that they are ''something fashioned,'' which is the original meaning of fictiō.

CONSTRUCTING NARRATIVES

When narrative is used to describe or represent an event, or events over time, the text—whether it is an article, dissertation, or book—is not the actual event, but rather a story about the event. The narrative is subsequent to what it tells. The paradox of narrative understanding is that we begin telling the story at the end of a lived experience. When we tell or write the story, we write backward from today. Our text is retroactively organized. Events take place in one direction, but we can tell about them only in the opposite direction. When we do so, we recollect, select, and reconstruct. Then we present and order our telling in a way that is consonant with the narrative structures and story forms that we are familiar with in our particular culture. In this way we ''make'' the story. When we acknowledge the constructed nature of our tellings, the line between real and literary narratives begins to blur.

We can see this blurring when we give close scrutiny to biographical and autobiographical writing. For the information on which their writing is based, biographers must rely on impressions left by their subjects and on records that are still available. The story of the life that biographers shape into text form comes out of those letters and documents about the biographical subject that chanced to be kept and out of those memories chosen to be shared. Biographers sift through all of these chance memories, artifacts, and impressions, discarding the trivial and reporting the significant. What counts as significant is largely determined by the conventions of the age in which the biographer lives. Cortazzi (1993) tells us that "a Western biographer or elicitor of autobiography may well be working within a cultural paradigm of the 'Great Man' tradition, where the story of a life is one of individual linear progress, a story of public achievement by a lone hero isolated from important social contexts, a story stressing the development of personality" (p. 21). Other peoples, having a group or a collective sense of self-identity, will not emphasize the individual at all. When asked, they will tell a different story of their lives. In this way, biography is a cultural construct. In this way, biographies are a "making." Roland Barthes once remarked that biographies are novels, although biographers would not care to have them called that; Barthes' own autobiography was a series of fragments, because he felt that a fragmented form was closer to the truth.

Autobiographies too are a fictiō, a making. Catholic in their confession, autobiographers promise truth and a verifiable identification between the author's name on the title page and the narrating self. But autobiographies are also retroactive in their organization. Events of the past are selected or rejected, presented or re-presented in keeping with the prescriptions of the genre. The result, as Rushdie (1991) suggests, is that " . . . we will not be capable of reclaiming precisely the thing that was lost; that we will, in short, create fictions, not actual cities or villages, but invisible ones, imaginary [ones]" (p. 10).

Different kinds of autobiographical writing foreground different elements of a life story, thereby veiling others. Operating out of the Platonic tradition that elevated thought over body, autobiographies have historically been an account of a spiritual quest. Therefore, the body in autobiographical writing has often been suppressed. Working-class autobiographies, however, are different. In these, introspection is replaced by testimonials of what the authors have accomplished and how they have accomplished it. Women's autobiographies exclude and embed different elements yet again. Heilbrun's (1988) work illustrates the way in which gender has been constructed in our society and how this has affected the way in which women are represented in biographical and autobiographical writing. Women writing about their own lives have historically suppressed aspects of their lives in order to make their stories conform to society's expectations of what their lives should be like. Within the construct of femininity, certain thoughts and experiences were unthinkable to tell. The expression of anger, the desire for power, or the need to gain control over one's life were beyond the bounds of social convention to acknowledge, and beyond the bounds of acceptable writing for women. Many stories were, therefore, never told. Consequently, as Virginia Woolf (in Heilbrun, 1988) noted, "very few women yet have written truthful autobiographies." And Heilbrun (1988) asks, "What secrets, what virtues, what passions, what discipline, what quarrels would, on the subject's death, be lost forever? How much would have vanished or been distorted or changed, even in our memories? We tell ourselves stories of our past, make fictions or stories of it, and these narrations *become* the past, the only part of our lives that is not submerged" (p. 51).

Although Raymond does not explore his own role in selecting memories to structure the story of his teaching, he is very concerned about issues of representation. In his journal response, he makes several references to facets of his story that were told, and those facets left untold. He worries that information was selected "at the expense of the way things really are" and that the picture of him was not whole, but partial and mediated. When we acknowledge the varying traditions and conventions that shape our writing, and understand the ways in which we retroactively construct our own stories, as well as the stories of others, then we can better understand James' and Raymond's stories as the fragments that Roland Barthes speaks of.

At another level, within whole disciplines such as history, what passes as history is the result of a similar process of selection, interpretation, and accommodation. It is impossible to tell everything that went on in a given time period, and so historians write about selected events that then become the facts of history. They choose to write about those themes that are significant. But what is significant is determined by culture and politics and further refined by the discipline itself. That is, what is significant will change if it is a military history, a social history, or an economic history. No two historians will say exactly the same thing about the same given events, even though both are attempting to give a true account. There is not one sole thing to be said about anything. There are many things that can be said. Because we cannot reclaim precisely all the happenings of the past, we construct different readings and writings of that past. White (1978/1989), pointing to the method of historical narrative itself, contends that "properly understood, histories ought never to be read as unambiguous signs of the events they report, but rather as symbolic structures, extended metaphors, that 'liken' the events reported in them to some form with which we have already become familiar in our literary culture" (p. 91). History views that which it describes from its own unique interpretive angle, and in the sense that historians unavoidably shape their accounts by rhetorical practices, history writing too is a form of literature.

Literary narratives are about events in a world that is made real to us through writing, and good writing can render this world newly strange. In the same way, narratives about real life can also serve to render the world newly strange. Rushdie (1991) explains it this way: "The point I want to make is that of course I'm not gifted with total recall, and it was precisely the partial nature of these memories, their fragmentation, that made them so evocative for me" (pp. 11–12). Compelling narratives about real life in the classroom can illuminate, can point outward beyond the circumstances of the events themselves to address more universal matters. The power and persuasiveness of the writing in narrative inquiry determine to a large extent whether it will be a penetrating or merely a pedestrian narrative. The persuasiveness, in turn, depends on how effectively the writer uses literary and rhetorical devices. Form and content are inextricably linked in this way.

Rhetorical Devices

Metaphor. Burke (1950) identified the four master tropes, or rhetorical devices, as metaphor, metonymy, synecdoche, and irony. White (1978/1989) argues that since synecdoche and metonymy are themselves forms of metaphor, there are in fact only two master tropes. Of these, metaphor is central to conveying meaning. Most people, however, view rhetorical devices at best as ornamental, at worst as hindrances to objective judgment. The centrality of metaphor is rejected by those who seek the kind of positive knowledge promised by the physical sciences. For many, metaphor is a device by which we obfuscate and deceive. But Lakoff and Johnson (1988) contend that "our ordinary conceptual system in terms of which we both think and act, is fundamentally metaphorical in nature" (p. 190). We think, act, and speak more or less automatically in our everyday life, unaware of the pervasiveness of metaphors and how they structure our perceptions and understandings. By looking at the language we use, we can begin to see how metaphors shape our views, our understandings, our expectations, and our actions. For example, thinking of marriage as a "contract agreement" leads to one set of expectations. Thinking of it as a "team effort" or as a "religious sacrament" carries different expectations. As another example, Lakoff and Johnson (1988) examine the way in which we structure, understand, and talk about arguments in terms of war. They cite the following examples to show the way in which the conceptual metaphor "argument is war" is reflected in our everyday language. In the familiar verbal battle of argument, we take up a position against our opponent, defend it, then win or lose the argument. We are next invited to set aside these belligerent military metaphors and to imagine a setting where argument is viewed as a dance. The participants, instead of attacking, defending, and counterattacking, would be intent on performing aesthetically pleasing movements. When argument is talked about in terms of dance, it is viewed and experienced differently.

Through language metaphors create an identity between things. When we speak of the classroom as a text, the classroom is metaphorically redescribed in terms of the frame of reference associated with written texts. Metaphors help us to understand one thing in terms of another. They can persuade us by saying that things we don't understand very well are really a lot like other things we know very well. In this way metaphors can make the strange familiar. White (1978/1989), writing about how tropes function in the discourse of the human sciences, argues that "troping is the soul of discourse, therefore the mechanism without which discourse cannot do its work or achieve its end" (p. 209). Further, he contends that although realistic discourse tries to disassociate itself from elements of style, from metaphors and figures of speech, "this flight, however, is futile; for tropics is the process by which all discourse *constitutes* the objects which it pretends only to describe realistically and to analyze objectively" (p. 208). No matter how mimetically a text intends to represent things as they are, there is always some slippage. White (1978/1989) writes that "on analysis, every mimesis can be shown to be distorted and can serve, therefore, as an occasion for yet another description of the same phenomenon, one claiming to be more realistic, more 'faithful to the facts'" (p. 210).

In our quest to describe the complexity of what we see and to tell about what we have come to know, we rely on metaphor. Let us look at the field of geography to illustrate our reliance on metaphor. Upon examination of the methods of geography, and in particular the work of cartographers in representing landscapes, we see that here, too, in this realistic discourse, rhetorical devices play a central role. Present-day cartography is a product of the Cartesian world in which the map is acknowledged as being a scaled representation of the real. It is held that a good map is one in which the image received by the map user corresponds to that intended by the map maker, and where the inscribed image is an accurate representation of the real world. Map making and map reading are seen to be a straightforward process of information transmission and retrieval. The commonly held belief is that cartography is an objective science, and that by the application of science, ever more precise representations of reality can be produced.

Harley (1992) challenges the belief that cartography is an objective science and illustrates the ways in which the values of ethnicity, politics, religion, and social class insert themselves into cartographic transcription. Much of the power of maps, Harley suggests, is that they operate behind a mask of seemingly neutral science. When we understand, however, the ways in which the tools of cartography are employed, we can begin to deconstruct the autonomy of the map and recognize its connection to the social world. Scale, size of symbols, thickness of lines, height of lettering, shading, and the addition of color all figure in the construction of a map. What the cartographer centers on the map or consigns to the margins adds force and meaning to the representation. Selection, omission, simplification, and classification all figure as steps in the map-making process, much as they do in the construction of a narrative. All these steps are inherently rhetorical.

By accepting the textuality of maps and their constructed nature, we are able to recognize what Harley (1992) describes as the "narrative qualities of cartographic representation" (p. 238). To illustrate the presence of metaphors and the intertextual dimension of maps, Harley (1992) cites the example of a contemporary state highway map of North Carolina. He begins by examining the margins of the map in this way:

> One side is taken up by an inventory of North Carolina points of interest—illustrated with photos of, among other things, a scimitar horned oryx (resident in the state zoo), a Cherokee woman making beaded jewelry, a ski lift, a sand dune (but no cities)—a ferry schedule, a message of welcome from the then governor, and a motorist's prayer ("Our heavenly Father, we ask this day a particular blessing as we take the wheel of our car . . . "). On the other side, North Carolina, hemmed in by the margins of pale yellow South Carolinas and Virginias, Georgias and Tennessees, and washed by a pale blue Atlantic, is represented as a meshwork of red, black, blue, green and yellow lines on a white background, thickened at the intersections by roundels of black or blotches of pink. . . . To the left of . . . [the] title is a sketch of the fluttering state flag. To the right is a sketch of a cardinal (state bird) on a branch of flowering dogwood (state flower) surmounting a buzzing honey bee arrested in midflight (state insect). (Wood & Fels, 1986, p. 54, in Harley, 1992, p. 240)

Harley reads the text of this map as follows: As an official highway map, the state of North Carolina has published it as a promotional device, and in this way the map has become an instrument of state policy. The map also constructs a mythic geography, a landscape full of points of interest, on which cities and towns are hierarchically arranged. The map underscores the values of Christianity and envelops the reader in state emblems of loyalty. Modern cartography, despite its claim of scientific accuracy, is an art of persuasive communication. It remains an inherently rhetorical discourse. For many, the term "rhetoric" is a pejorative term, linked to propaganda mapping or advertising. But Harley's (1992) position "is to accept that rhetoric is part of the way all texts work and that all maps are rhetorical texts" (p. 242). Thus rhetorical analysis, until recently applied mainly to literary texts, is indispensable for reading any kind of discourse.

White and Epston (1990) provide another example as they explain the way in which they employ narrative in the field of family therapy, and how they help their patients to reauthor their lives through the use of new and different metaphors. After each meeting with a client, Epston writes letters to the client. These letters constitute his notes for the session, and by sharing these notes as letters, he hopes to establish a more egalitarian relationship between therapist and client. In language reminiscent of Clandinin and Connelly's writing, White and Epston describe therapy as a process of storying and re-storying in which the letters function as a tool in the co-creation of new, liberating narratives for those seeking help. In everyday life, as in a therapy setting, we ascribe meaning to our lives by plotting our experiences into stories. These stories then shape our lives and relationships. Some stories are filled with strong images that promote competence and wellness. Some stories are metaphorically uplifting, liberating, and healing. Others, however, serve to constrain, trivialize, or otherwise pathologize ourselves and our relationships. The particular story that prevails or dominates in giving meaning to the events of our lives determines to a large extent the nature of our lived experiences and our patterns of action. White and Epston (1990) explore ways in which they can enable the writing of stories that liberate and heal, ways in which people can reauthor their lives through the use of new and different metaphors. In this way, our natural inclination to live by metaphors is harnessed as a tool for change.

Narrative synecdoche. Let us now examine how we use rhetorical devices at the story level as we construct our narratives of the classroom. At the story level, we can refer to what we tell as narrative synecdoche. Synecdoche is a form of metaphor, a figure of speech in which the part stands for the whole or, conversely, the whole stands for a part. In "Give us this day our daily bread," bread stands for the meals taken each day. Thus something else is understood within the thing mentioned. Synecdoche is common in everyday speech, too. In the news headline "MOSCOW'S NEW BOSS," Moscow represents the whole of Russia. "The Crown" represents the monarchy, "The Bench" the judiciary, and "The Stage" the theatrical profession. When we tell stories of teaching, these stories are only a part of the whole classroom experience, and an even smaller part of the teacher's total life. The narratives are bounded by time and place and simplified through the ordering process of telling. Nevertheless, the details contained in the telling are meant to convey to us a sense of the whole. In this way, classroom narratives are synecdochic.

Similarly, photographers in their work rely on visual synecdoche, hoping that a small part of a scene will suggest the whole. A crying child, barren fields in the background, an emaciated mother—these are presented to suggest the pain of a famine-ravaged country. Much information is conveyed in these photographic images, but much is also hidden from our view. The photographer's lens has captured only one part of the story, one moment in time, fixed in a small and unmoving frame. No directions are given as to how these images should be read. There are no instructions and no rules for understanding the purpose of the picture, the context, the selection, or inclusion procedures of the photographer. If we are to understand the images, we must do the work of reading ourselves.

Our job as readers means that we write for ourselves those parts of the story left out. We fill in the gaps of the text, whether photographic or narrative. As Eco (1979) explains, "frequently, given a series of causally and linearly connected events $a \ldots e$, a text tells the reader about the event a and, after a while, about the event e, taking for granted that the reader has already anticipated the dependent events b, c, d" (pp. 214–215). Based on the cues that the text provides, readers compose these dependent events. In this way, readers become active participants in constructing the meaning of a text. Given the partiality of stories, their synecdochic nature, each reader will make them satisfyingly whole in different ways. In this way, narrative, although it says less than it knows, often makes known more than it says (Genette, 1980). We can never hope to capture in our narratives the full richness and complexity of our lived-through classroom experiences. The ups and downs of classroom work, the cross-currents of thought and feeling cannot all be conveyed, so we make decisions about which parts will stand for the whole. How do we manage this partiality so that it carries for the reader implications of the whole?

L'effet de réel. Part of our task is to order the words and events within the story in such a way that readers can make meaningful connections within the text. This ordering is in large part culturally determined. Cortazzi (1993) cites the following examples that point to the vast range of cultural variation possible in the internal structuring of narratives. In the Kuna language of Panama, a narrator may jump back and forth from place to place, in what we would find to be an incomprehensible and illogical manner. In the Tharu language of Nepal, events are always presented in order of occurrence, thereby ruling out flashbacks. In Dan, of Liberia, no two events in narrative can happen simultaneously, only sequentially. The Arapaho, a Native American tribe, believe that life is eternal, and this view is represented in their narrative structure through stories that are most often serial, without definite endings. We write our teachers' stories from within our narrative conventions, too. Most often this means that we seek out turning points and ask how they came to be. We value childhood events, as these are part of the whole story. We inquire into motives and the meaning of events. We document struggles and tensions. Then we arrange these in chronological order. American Indian narratives, in contrast, usually hold childhood episodes as irrelevant. Their narratives are little concerned with chronology, and are apt to be episodic. Thus, narrative structures reflect cultural ways of telling.

Within the conventions of qualitative research writing in our academic communities, we are often introduced to figurative language even as we pick up a study to read titles such as this one: ''The past as prologue: A qualitative study of the roles of biography and teachers' beliefs in the practice of teaching.'' The content of the study is evoked by the words before the colon, then explained by the words that follow the colon. As in all narratives, titles function as markers to indicate the beginning of a text. We are then drawn into the story by the writer's use of concrete details. These create a sense of the setting, making it come alive and seem real for the reader. Roland Barthes (1977) refers to this as *l'effet de réel*. Detailed descriptions of people, their actions, and the settings in which these have taken place allow us to envision the persons and the classrooms. Details bring out the uniqueness and individuality of the teachers in our narratives. As readers of these narratives, we do not encounter statistical abstracts of the average teacher. Instead, the teachers and the experiences of their classrooms come alive for us in such a way that, although they may not be our experiences, we can relate to their situatedness and understand them.

In fictional narratives, readers get to know characters by the things the characters say, by the things they do, and by what others say about them. We come to know the teachers in school narratives through these same means. The struggles and tensions of the classroom are defined, and we as readers interpret and draw conclusions, as we have done with James' and Raymond's stories. Conversations between teachers and researchers are dissolved and condensed into indirect discourse.

Insights are called forth through the trope of irony. In our stories of the classroom, the oxymoron of the observer-participant is understood and accepted. Our stories are located in time, but temporal distortions in the narrative are common. One year of a teacher's life might be summed up in two sentences, or conversely, several pages can be devoted to the description of a momentary experience. When the intended audience for our stories is the academic community, we also cite the work of other authors to give legitimacy and weight to our own writing. All the selected events of the research experience are then drawn together to meet the rudimentary requirements of story as we know it: a beginning, with intervening events, followed by an ending.

In these and many other ways, the writers of qualitative research texts use literary and rhetorical conventions much as the authors of fictional narratives do when they construct their texts. The process of narrating is a way of ordering, and this very sense of order and closure that the narrative conveys gives authority to the text. It becomes the role of the reader then to interrogate the text in order to understand the partiality and managed nature of the narrative. Both the novel and the texts of narrative inquiry are modes of representing reality. What unites real stories with the stories of fiction is their mutual dependence on narrative discourse and the conventions of the narrative to order and communicate events in such a way that the reader can draw meaning from those events. When we read a novel we transcend its pages, and are drawn into the lives and experiences of its characters. The narratives of teachers' lives and classroom experiences invite us to respond in a similar way. The vividness of narrative research accounts, achieved through the use of rhetorical devices, brings the teacher and classroom to life for us. As we read, we can visualize the activities and feel the tensions. The story becomes real and we can say, "Ah yes, that's right. That's how it is." Literary theory can help us to understand how writing creates these effects and how reading achieves them. Literary theory can help us to understand how we can enter into texts in different ways, and how we respond to the textual representations of research work.

Literary Theories

Striking similarities exist among key concepts that have emerged recently in the fields of physics, economics, psychology, medicine, reading, and literary theory. Although the mechanistic paradigm still dominates our everyday thinking, quantum physics long ago demonstrated the limitations of this paradigm. Weaver (1985) describes for the nonscientist developments in quantum physics that parallel developments in the fields of reading and literary theory. In 1803 Thomas Young confirmed the hypothesis that light has the properties of a wave. In 1905 Albert Einstein demonstrated that light has the properties of a particle. Since no one has been able to disprove either conclusion, light is understood to be both a wave and a particle. For quantum physics, the wave-particle duality marked the end of an either-or way of understanding the world. If light is observed by means of the double-slit experiment Young used, then it is a wave. If light is observed using the photoelectric effect that Einstein used, then it is a particle. We as observers can thus have light be either a wave or a particle, depending on how we choose to observe it. What it will be depends on our transaction with light. Even as we choose one method of observation, we forego a view of its other property. The belief that things are what they are, regardless of how we observe them, can then no longer be defended. The observer and the observed are inseparable. While the mechanistic paradigm has led to magnificent insights and achievements, it is generally acknowledged that fundamentally the nature of the universe is more like an organism, a process with no clear separation between subjective and objective, observer and observed.

A parallel shift away from a mechanistic, toward an organic, paradigm has also occurred in thinking about literature. The term "New Criticism" defines the critical theory that emerged in the 1920s and dominated Anglo-American literary criticism for decades thereafter. New Criticism was an affirmation of positivism. New Criticism held that every text was autonomous and that history, biography, sociology, psychology, authors' intentions, and readers' private experiences were all irrelevant to the reading of a text. New Criticism argued that the text was a stable, meaning-bearing entity. There was a wholeness to texts. Each text had a central unity, and there was one correct reading of any given literary work. The author's intentions and the reader's individual responses to the work were thought to be irrelevant in achieving a perfect reading of the work and determining its meaning. The New Critics looked for objective readings of a text, uncontaminated by the personality of the individual doing the reading. Until recently, alternatives to these New Criticism interpretive strategies were regarded with suspicion. Now, however, we no longer try to maintain a dispassionate objectivity, a sense of separation between self and other, between self and text. From the viewpoint of contemporary criticism, the New Critical notion of a detached observer—an epistemologically innocent bystander—no longer exists. Rather, postmodern criticism posits complete involvement between reader and text. New Criticism no longer dominates the way we think about texts. Instead, contemporary criticism promotes a new paradigm and a radically new mode of comprehension. Unity and wholeness in a text have now been relegated to the periphery of critical concern, at the same time that erudition has been replaced by interrogation and interpretation of the text.

Although New Criticism contributed much to our understanding of texts, and still provides for us one avenue of entry into texts, reading is far too rich and many-faceted an activity to be exhausted by any single theory. Postmodern theories of criticism now span a wide and often bewildering spectrum of approaches to texts. The discourse of literature and literary theory seems to be everywhere. We encounter it in architecture, law, history, geography, feminist studies, political science, philosophy, and theology. Not surprisingly, it has also entered the discourse of education. Common to the many different theories of contemporary literary criticism is a general privileging of the role of the reader and the challenge to read the world and the word in different ways, to look at how the meaning in texts is constructed and to think about how we as readers relate to texts. We frequently encounter Bakhtin on the pages of education research articles and books. As a literary theorist, Bakhtin's exploration of dialogicality, voices, social languages, and reported speech has given us new understandings about the ways in which we use oral and written language. Bakhtin (1981) tells us that the univocal text is not possible, that it is not possible to speak of a single unaltered meaning or message; that all "transcription systems including the speaking voice in a living utterance—are inadequate to the multiplicity of the meanings they seek to convey. My voice gives the illusion of unity to what I say; I am, in fact, *constantly* expressing a plenitude of meanings, some intended, others of which I am unaware" (p. xx). Roland Barthes also speaks of the plural voices of the text and describes the voice of the author as a weaving of other voices. The goal of reading, he tells us, is not to uncover a single, fixed, and correct interpretation. This is impossible, for the text is endlessly open. Rather, the goal of reading is to free as many varied and perhaps conflicting meanings as the text might suggest.

Here we are drawn back to Raymond's specific concerns of representation, as well as more general concerns about acceptable ways of presenting and responding to research texts. Raymond's quest for the one right and whole reading of his classroom practice stands at odds with a reading process that seeks to set free a multiplicity of meanings. We no longer carry a vision of scientific inquiry leading to a unity of knowledge, nor do we seek unity and wholeness in a text. Just as I read the text of Raymond's classroom differently from the way in which he read, or wanted to have his classroom practices read, subsequent readers also responded to the written narrative in different ways. Their responses were not shaped by research conclusions transmitted in a scientifically rational, distanced, writing style. Instead, readers were drawn into the body of the teachers' stories. They could visualize the settings. They sensed and felt the classroom tensions. They became part of the process of making the meaning. They responded to the teachers as people and came away, each with different understandings.

We do not have a long tradition of making teachers' stories public. We are not used to noting the similarities that the texts of teachers' stories share with the texts of fictional stories. We also do not have a long history of responding to teachers' stories as we would respond to other authors' works. But the value of examining the constructedness of narratives in education and using literary theories to gain a greater understanding of the texts of narrative inquiry is apparent for all texts, those authored solely by researchers as well as those collaboratively authored. In the process of telling stories, we order our knowing. We reframe or re-create through the stories we tell. We do not write as if on a mountaintop viewing and recording the scene below, from a privileged vantage point. We also do not look into texts from outside. We do both our reading and our writing from within a situated world. The way in which teachers tell their stories is faithful to certain narrative conventions, and the way in which these stories are reported and find their way into written texts is also faithful to the narrative conventions of the particular community within which the stories appear. The way in which the reading community responds to a text and to the relationship between author and discourse is also dependent on the situational variables of time and place. Foucault (1989) explains that originally discourse was an act before it became a product caught up in ownership and attributable to an individual author. When we read the texts of other people's stories, literary theories can help us to reconsider issues of ownership, voice, and authorship. Literary theories address the many ways in which readers enter into oral texts, written texts, or the texts of the classroom and the ways in which they reframe and recreate the stories therein.

The author's role. During the Middle Ages, literary texts such as narratives, epics, and tragedies were circulated and accepted without any reference to their author. An author's name was not deemed necessary, and the anonymity of the author seemed to cause no difficulty for readers. On the other hand, scientific texts of the Middle Ages were accepted as true only when these were marked with the author's name, as in "Hippocrates said." Foucault (1989) tells us that "The coming into being of the notion of the 'author' constitutes the privileged moment of *individualization* in the history of ideas, knowledge, literature, philosophy, and the sciences" (p. 263). By the seventeenth or eighteenth century, Foucault continues, a reversal occurred. The author's function in scientific texts faded away: "Scientific discourses began to be received for themselves, in the anonymity of an established or always redemonstrable truth; their membership in a systematic ensemble, and not the reference to the individual who produced them, stood as their guarantee" (p. 268). The inventor's or author's name served merely to identify a particular theorem. In literature, too, a reversal in author function occurred. Meaning, status, and value of a text now became dependent on answers to questions of who wrote it, when, and under what circumstances. In concluding his discussion of the ways in which author function and status have changed over time, Foucault (1989) predicts that:

> As our society changes, at the very moment when it is in the process of changing, the author function will disappear. . . .
> All discourses, whatever their status, form, value, and whatever the treatment to which they will be subjected, would then develop in the anonymity of a murmur. We would no longer hear the questions that have been rehashed for so long: Who really spoke? Is it really he and not someone else? With what authenticity or originality? And what part of his deepest self did he express in this discourse? Instead, there would be other questions, like these: What are the modes of existence of this discourse? Where has it been used, how can it circulate, and who can appropriate it for himself? (p. 275)

Barthes (1968/1989) also addresses the question of the function of the author in an essay entitled "The Death of the Author." He, too, contends that the "author" is a recent creation produced by our society as it emerged out of the Middle Ages. He speculates that positivism has granted the greatest importance to the author's person, and that this was then consolidated by the New Criticism. Assigning an author to a text brings that text to a halt, closes the writing, as it were. This is quite suited to classical criticism, which then goes about discovering the author and explaining the text. For Barthes, a text does not consist of a line of words releasing a single message from the author. Rather, he speaks of the openness of a text, of its plural voices, no one of which is more important or authentic than the other. He sees the text not as an object, but rather as something held in language, and experienced only in the activity of reading. Barthes reminds us of the etymological origin of the word *text* as something woven out of separate strands, and speaks of the reading process as an unraveling of these strands. He advocates a systematic study of narrative to show that the meaning of a text does not preexist in the text, but is dependent on the codes that are operative in every text. Meaning is thus generated in the process of textual analysis, and the goal of reading, of textual analysis, is never to uncover a single, fixed, and correct interpretation. It is not possible to find a single meaning when the text is conceived, as Barthes (1968/1989) maintains, of ''a multi dimensional space in which are married and contested several writings, none of which is original: the text is a fabric of quotations, resulting from a thousand sources of culture'' (p. 57). The goal of reading is, rather, the freeing of as many varied and perhaps conflicting meanings as the text might suggest. Barthes tells us that the reader should never be a mere consumer of text, one who merely processes words and reads as denotatively as possible. Instead of being submissive to the text, being mere consumers of the text, Barthes urges readers to play with the text, to manipulate it, and to question it. In doing so, not all the meanings of a text will be released. This is impossible because ''the text is open ad infinitum: no reader, no subject, no science can exhaust the text. . . . '' (Barthes, 1977, p. 1). But in the process of unraveling the interwoven strands of the text, the reader comes to a deeper understanding of how meaning is possible, of how the text bursts forth.

Barthes read the texts of news items, photographs, wrestling matches, and town plans as closely as he read the texts of fiction. All invite textual analysis. He made no distinction between fictive and nonfictive texts, arguing that distinctions between literary writing and writing outside literature were quite dated. He argued that instead of using the term ''literature,'' it would be better to say ''writing,'' and he advocated an active role for the reader in response to writing. His goal was for the reader to become the producer of text. He rejected what had been the accepted reading stance, saying, ''Our literature is characterized by the pitiless divorce which the literary institution maintains between the producer of the text and its user, between its owner and its customer, between its author and its reader. This reader is thereby plunged into a kind of idleness—he is intransitive; he is in short *serious*: instead of functioning himself, instead of gaining access to the magic of the signifier, to the pleasure of writing, he is left with no more than the poor freedom either to accept or reject the text: reading is nothing more than a *referendum*'' (in Rosenblatt, 1978, p. 169).

Privileging the reader's voice. Envisioning a new role for the reader, Barthes (1968/1989) tells us that although texts consist of multiple writings, ''There is a site where this multiplicity is collected, and this site is not the author, as has been hitherto claimed, but the reader; the reader is the very space in which are inscribed, without any of them being lost, all the citations out of which a writing is made; the unity of a text is not in its origin but in its destination" (p. 59). With the death of what Barthes calls the positivist myth of the "author" comes the liberation of the reader, who becomes the creator of meaning. In this way authority is given to those who read the texts of teachers' classrooms and those who read teachers' stories in textual form.

Many of Barthes' ideas, so strikingly and quixotically expressed, are congenial to the ideas expressed by Reader Response theorists. Reader Response theories explore the complex relationship of how readers are either moved or not moved to participate in the rhetorical devices meant to engage them. The privileging of the role of the reader is the central tenet of Reader Response criticism. Within the designation of Reader Response criticism, there are numerous complex theories that cover a vast area of the critical landscape, theories that occasionally shift in their emphasis, and often conflict, yet also frequently overlap. What unites these numerous positions is a common interest in the role of the reader, and the realization that various dimensions of interpretation in reading are possible. Suleiman and Crosman (1980) identify six contemporary approaches to Reader Response criticism. At one end of the continuum are those response theorists who see readers as more or less passive, their responses controlled by the text. At the other end of the continuum are critics who view readers as the active creators of meaning, and see the text as secondary, passive, or even nonexistent as an objective work. The middle ground between these positions is held by critics who see reading as a process of co-creative text production involving some interactive combination of the reader and the text. Rosenblatt's (1938/1976, 1978) transactional theory of the literary work falls into this middle category. Her 1938 publication, *Literature as Exploration*, is often credited with being the first formulation of Reader Response theory, although it had little impact on literary theory until 30 years later. Rosenblatt challenged the objectivist assumptions of the New Criticism as they affected the reading and teaching of literary works. She challenged the notion of the work as an object, a static set of meaning existing "out there" for the reader and critic to illuminate. She argued instead that "a text, once it leaves its author's hands, is simply paper and ink until a reader evokes from it a literary work—sometimes, even, a literary work of art" (Rosenblatt, 1978, p. ix). Rosenblatt first proposed the term *transaction* to describe the relationship between reader and text in which both the reader and the text influence and shape the meaning that emerges. What we as readers bring to the text influences what we will make of it.

There seems to be a natural kinship or connection between the process of transaction as it is defined in Reader Response theory and "collaboration" as the term is used to describe the relationship between research partners in collaborative narrative inquiry. Rosenblatt (1988) intended the term *transaction* to be used to "designate relationships in which each element conditions and is conditioned by the other in a mutually-constituted situation" (p. 2). Transaction thus carries the same interfusion of elements, the same blending of components, and the same overtones of mutuality central to effective collaboration. The term *transaction* describes the collaborative relationship between reader and text, the unique coming together of a particular personality and a particular text at a particular time and place through which meaning is evoked. Rosenblatt (1978) explains the creative transaction between thought and language this way:

> The poem, then, must be thought of as an event in time. It is not an object or an ideal entity. It happens during a coming together, a compenetration of a reader and a text. The reader brings to the text his past experience and present personality. Under the magnetism of the ordered symbols of the text, he marshals his resources and crystallizes out from the stuff of memory, thought, and feeling a new order, a new experience which he sees as the poem. This becomes part of the ongoing stream of his life experience, to be reflected on from any angle important to him as a human being. (p. 12)

Rosenblatt uses the term "poem" to mean any literary work. The text itself, however, is not the literary work. As the reader transacts with the words created by the writer, the reader's feelings, ideas, and beliefs are modified, and the poem or literary work is simultaneously created. This evocation of the poem is an event in time. Changing the circumstances of reader, place, and time will produce a different event, a different poem. Although the text is essential, to bring the poem into being, a reader is required. Making meaning involves both the text and what the reader brings to the text. The poem, the novel, or the story comes into being during the aesthetic transaction. The lived-through current of ideas, images, and tensions becomes shaped into what the reader sees as the evocation corresponding to the text. This is what the reader starts reacting or responding to during the reading event. Interpretation is then an analysis of the work that readers themselves have called forth.

Efferent and aesthetic reading. Rosenblatt's early work focused primarily on the aesthetic reading of literary works of art, but she also discusses the reader's active role in efferent reading. In aesthetic reading the reader's attention is centered on the aesthetic experience of the lived-through fusion with the text. In efferent reading, the reader's attention is drawn to the information to be acquired from the text. The term "efferent" comes from the Latin, "to carry away." The reading of a scientific text or a newspaper article from which the reader will carry away information is thus generally considered to be efferent reading. The distinction between "efferent" and "aesthetic" depends on what the reader does. In the past, the tendency has been to assume that such a distinction depends entirely on the text involved, because the character of the work was held to be inherent in the text. In actuality, the distinction depends on what stance the reader adopts, either consciously or unconsciously, toward a text. At the extreme efferent end of the spectrum, readers would bracket the personal and qualitative elements of their response, concentrating only on the information left when the reading is over. At the aesthetic end of the spectrum, the reader's primary purpose is fulfilled in the lived-through experiencing of the text. Although reading a poem is an aesthetic activity, we can shift easily in our reading of poetry to an efferent appreciation of the poet's skillful use of imagery. Similarly, a scientist can shift unconsciously to an aesthetic stance, savoring the elegance of a complex equation. In actual fact, Rosenblatt (1978) acknowledges that

> no hard-and-fast line separates efferent—scientific or expository—reading on the one hand from aesthetic reading on the other. It is more accurate to think of a continuum, a series of gradations between the nonaesthetic and the aesthetic extremes. The reader's stance toward the text—what he focuses his attention on, what his "mental set" shuts out or permits to enter into the center of awareness—may vary in a multiplicity of ways between the two poles. (p. 35)

A sentence or a paragraph in Bronte's *Jane Eyre* (1847/1985) will evoke different images and different responses in different readers. Similarly, a reading of Rachel Carson's *Silent Spring*, undertaken as an efferent reading in search of verifiable ecological information, also invites a range of aesthetic responses generated by the words and their referents. Variations in reader response during primarily efferent reading are illustrated by MacLean's (1986) case study of the different ways in which fluent readers interact with expository texts. Three schoolteachers participated in MacLean's study and were required to read expository texts that they could comprehend with ease. MacLean noted the following different patterns of reader text interaction: One reader tended to integrate text in terms of her own personal experience. She elaborated on and reconstructed the meaning of the text in such a way that although it was not completely inconsistent with the text, it extended considerably from the text. The second reader tended to be very textbound, generating mostly text-centered responses. The third reader could be situated somewhere in the middle of the continuum between the first two. MacLean concluded that individuals with comparable reading skills do not process expository text in the same way.

Thus, we see that both fictive and nonfictive texts offer multiple possibilities for readers' responses. It is the readers who draw selectively, although not necessarily consciously, on their own fund of knowledge, experience, and personality to respond in their own way to the verbal symbols on the page. Iser (1978) maintains that a successful reading of any text "depends on the extent to which this text can activate the individual reader's faculties of perceiving and processing. . . . Of course, the text is a 'structured prefigurement' but that which is given has to be received, and the way in which it is received depends as much on the reader as on the text" (p. 107). Because no story can ever be told in its entirety, a text always leaves gaps in the telling of a story, which readers must fill, and which individual readers fill in different ways. For this reason, every text is potentially capable of several different realizations.

We are moving away from old paradigms toward new ways of understanding the world around us. We are changing our methods of research and inquiry into the classroom, but for the most part, we still continue to read the written texts of our research inquiries in the old ways. Texts, through their rhetoric, guide us as we read them, but we are also trapped by the conventions we have been taught about reading, to read in certain ways. When we read a detective story, we expect to look for certain things such as mysterious events, clues, close calls, and vulnerable victims. Faced with science fiction, we prepare to exercise "a willing suspension of disbelief." When we see a poem, the form of the poem itself suggests that we are going to encounter a particular kind of text. In the same way, the dissertation form and the research article suggest certain reading conventions, too. The title, the abstract, and the opening sentences help to establish the work as serious, and in response to these cues we adopt a certain reading stance. Faced with a research text, we tend to adopt a reading stance that denies our interaction with the text and privileges the text as a meaning bearing entity, transmitting its meaning to the reader, a more or less passive consumer of text. What would happen if we suspended these reading conventions?

Making meaning. As readers, we do not merely consume the texts of qualitative research studies and read them efferently. The vivid descriptions of narrative inquiry, bringing to life the events of the class-room and the teacher's work, invite our response. As readers, we savor the qualities of the structured ideas, situations, scenes, personalities, and emotions called forth, participating in the tensions, conflicts, and resolutions as they unfold. According to the theorists occupying the middle ground of Reader Response theory, the character of a work does not inhere entirely in the text. The visual display of the text, the marks on the page, provide only a fraction of the information to a reader. We as readers also make contributions. No writing system can bring all aspects of what is said into our awareness. We will always encounter gaps. We can transcribe what was said, but not how it was said, or how the speaker wanted the listener to take what was said. What is lost in the transcription is what is difficult to recover in the act of reading. As Eco (1979) points out, "Texts are lazy machineries that ask someone to do part of their job" (p. 214). It is the reader's job to fill in the gaps in a text.

While Iser views the text as a prefigured structure within which the reader makes meaning and Rosenblatt sees reading as a co-creative process of text production, the subjective critics David Bleich and Nor-man Holland share the conviction that books do not have meaning; people do. Bleich (1975) considers the role of the text in reading as secondary, and Holland (1975) describes the text as passive. Holland maintains that readers re-create texts, as it were, according to their own personalities. Holland came to this conclusion after giving the students he was working with projective personality tests as a way of establishing identity themes for the students. Then he asked students for free associations to stories he gave them to read. In doing so, he discovered that the text almost vanished in the astounding variability of different readers' re-creation of it. Although the text remained the same, everyone responded to it differently. For Holland, the question was not which is the better reading, but rather, what is the something in each character that makes their perception of the story different? Holland found that there was a significant correlation between the readers' free associations and their personalities, and concluded that interpretation is a function of the reader's identity.

Holland believes that although individuals might change over time, their identity theme remains the same. There may be variations on this central theme, and it may be expressed differently, but nevertheless, Holland believes, one central theme characterizes all aspects of an individual's life. Texts pass through the filter of each reader's personality, and readers respond to a literary work by projecting onto it and by taking from it that which is compatible with their identity theme. If readers respond positively to a work, or to parts of it, it is because the text is compatible with their identity theme. Alternatively, if readers have no reaction to a literary work, or a negative one, then they have not been able to incorporate or adapt the work in such a way as to be compatible with their personal theme. Coles (1989) expressed a similar view when he said, "Remember, what you are hearing is to some considerable extent a function of *you*, hearing" (p. 15). In the classroom and in the reading of factual texts such as curriculum documents, the reading transaction as Holland describes it might occur as discussed in Chapter Three.

Holland's theory of reader response is only one of many theories, each of which offers us new insights into how we enter into texts and collaborate with them to make meaning. As with all theories, Holland's psychoanalytic approach to reading also invites criticism. He has been criticized for rejecting as an oversimplification the notion that a text has unity, but nevertheless finding the unity that he rejected in the text within the reader. Despite criticisms of Holland's theory, his model does have something to offer to theorists of reading. Holland has contributed very extensive case histories and protocols of readers reading and has reminded us that reading is not only an interpersonal and institutionalized enterprise, but also a private phenomenon.

Gadamer (1960) offers us another insight into the personal process of reading. According to Gadamer, the meaning of a text is never fixed, but is always changing as a result of our interpretations. We interpret texts within a horizon. When we read a text, we apply it to our present situation. This results in a fusion of horizons, in which the perspective of text and reader are combined into a new and broader horizon. In the same way, when we tell stories about past experiences, Gadamer says, the experience and the story communicate with one another and in this process of fusion, both the experience and the story get a new meaning.

The various critical theorists understand the process of reading and meaning-making differently and invite us as readers onto divergent paths of textual interrogation. Roland Barthes advocates a systematic process of analysis, urging readers to search out the cultural codes that he sees operative in every text. Rosenblatt describes the reader as adopting a particular reading stance, either predominantly efferent or primarily aesthetic. It is this stance that gives shape to the meanings made as the reader transacts with a text. In Rosenblatt's terms, the text is the blueprint from which we "perform" the poem. Similarly, Iser sees the text as the guide for our various personal realizations of meaning. Holland, on the other hand, suggests that readers make meaning by re-creating texts according to their own personalities. And Gadamer visualizes the process of interpreting texts across a shifting horizon of meaning.

Within the many different critical frameworks that guide reading and interpretation, there are some commonly agreed-upon precepts. There is a newly defined appreciation of the role of the reader. As readers give voice to the marks on the page, they bring to life the events in the text and give meaning to them.

The vast array of reading possibilities offered to us by literary theorists gives us a greater appreciation of the many ways in which meaning can be realized from the texts of James' and Raymond's stories. It is also generally recognized that the study of texts is not limited to books. Textual studies have pushed well beyond the page and the book to encompass a myriad of other sign systems. The constructed nature of these systems has been studied and probed, and consequently our erstwhile distinctions between what is fact and what is fiction have been questioned and opened for examination in different ways. Culler (1982) has also observed that within the different positions that reading and literary theorists assume, the relationship between reader and text is invariably organized around issues of control, objectivity, and mastery. Debate revolves around questions such as what is "in" the text. How can we distinguish what the text supplies from what the reader contributes? Does the text control readers, or do readers manipulate the text to produce meanings that suit their own interests?

Iser's response to these questions would be that although the reader is actively involved in filling in the gaps of a text, it is the text that provides the limiting structure within which the reader shapes the work. Stanley Fish (1980) maintains that there is no objective work of literature. In his view, reading is the process of experiencing what the text does to you. For Holland and Bleich, the subjective critics, readers hold the controlling interest in the enterprise of reading. Holland sees the text as passive. Bleich describes reading as a wholly subjective process in which the text is secondary and the personality of the reader determines the nature of what is perceived. Rosenblatt objects to this overemphasis on the reader's personality, and on the question of whether reading is text- or reader-dominated. She chooses a middle ground, describing reading as a co-creative process.

Whether the text leads the reader toward an ending or the reader manipulates the text to its conclusion, in both cases we have also come to expect that upon closing the covers of a book we will have reached a degree of mastery as our experience of reading turns into knowledge. Holland (in Belenky et al., 1986) captures the importance we place on mastery, as revealed in our need to get things right: "Our concern about interpreting wrongly, about being limited in what we can see or understand of a work . . . proceeds from the debilitating assumption that each of us experiences something imperfectly and someone else knows just how imperfectly'' (p. 222).

The sense of getting it right, of mastering a text, might be defined in Barthes' terms as the experience of the readerly text. The readerly text is a text we know how to read. It has a certain transparency. It will affirm things we already know and values we already have, thus leaving us undisturbed. Faced with what Barthes calls a readerly text, the reader responds as a consumer, restricted to producing the intended meaning enshrined in the text by the author. What is infinitely more desirable, insisted Barthes, is to experience the writerly text. The writerly text is resistant to passive reading. A writerly text will in some way disrupt our settled expectations. A writerly text engages readers in active play with its many threads as readers unravel the threads to make not one, but many meanings. The variety of interpretations to which a narrative text lends itself and the variety of reader responses to that text result in an infinitely large number of readings.

A 17th-century English court, upon delivering a legal decision, declared that once released into public territory, a text is inevitably subject to whatever interpretation seems most plausible to its readers, who will determine its meaning in the light of local circumstances. Several centuries later, Barthes (1977) makes a similar assertion, writing that ''narration can only receive its meaning from the world which makes use of it'' (p. 115). The meaning of a text, then, depends on the way in which we use it. The meaning depends on the interpretive strategies we bring to it, the questions we choose to ask of it, the stance we take toward it, and the connections we are particularly interested in making. As Rosenblatt reminds us, the relationship between reader and text is a unique coming together of a particular personality and a particular text at a particular time and place under particular circumstances. Every change of community, time, place, purpose, or circumstance will effect a different transaction with a text.

Reading collaboratively. Biology textbooks are read in a predominantly efferent reading fashion. Poetry, on the other hand, is read for a different purpose. It invites an aesthetic reading stance. Reading poetry efferently is counterproductive. It is not a reading stance sympathetic to that kind of writing. In the culture of our reading community, we do not find it purposeful to enter into the reading of poetry with the intention of coming away from that reading with a series of facts in hand. Instead, when we encounter poetry we adopt an attitude of readiness to focus our attention on what is being lived through during the reading event. Let us examine now the purpose and circumstances of our reading of the narratives of collaborative inquiry. What stance is appropriate to adopt as we transact with the texts of narrative inquiry? Should mastery and control figure strongly in our reading stance? Or is a collaborative interpretive stance more resonant with the purpose of the research and the tone of the writing? Schweickart's (1989) feminist approach to reading and her discussion of purpose in reading provide a starting point for our response to these questions and the consideration of a reader–text relationship that is collaborative and dialogic in nature.

As was discussed in Chapter 5, fidelity and caring characterize collaborative narrative inquiry relationships, which are founded on trust and fostered through conversation. Care is taken to negotiate meanings throughout the inquiry process, to portray the people involved and to inscribe their voices in the text in confirming ways. The research is intended to describe and foster understanding of teachers and classroom practices. It is research conducted differently from the way it has traditionally been done, and so it warrants a different way of responding. It is research and writing situated within an ethic of caring, and so it invites a reading sympathetic to the intention of the writing. What unites fiction with narrative inquiry is their mutual dependence on rhetorical devices and narrative conventions to order events and convey them to readers in meaningfully storied ways. What distinguishes narrative inquiry from fiction is that in the former the events recorded took place and involved real people with real feelings. The reader encounters not just a text, but a real person within the lived story of the narrative inquiry. Schweickart (1989) sees the process of reading as the reader seeking to connect, understand, and be in relationship with the existence behind the text. This focus on the dialogical, on conversation, and on relationship echoes the writings of Buber and Noddings, and evokes the characteristic elements of collaborative inquiry. It also brings to the fore the notions of fidelity and caring that lie at the heart of collaborative narrative inquiry. A lived story calls for space to come to the reading of that story with an attitude of care. Creating a space within the reading framework to incorporate an attitude of caring and connecting to the other within the text establishes a different perspective from which to read the research story. Within a dialogic model of reading, the purpose is not to analyze a text as object in order to gain mastery over it, but rather to connect with the existence behind the text. In this way, Connelly and Clandinin (1990) suggest, research stories help us to "learn something essentially human by understanding an actual life or community as lived'' (p. 8). In this way the dialectic of control gives way to the dialectic of communication.

Adopting a caring stance does not fix or direct the meaning that will be realized in the reading. That will remain culturally, historically, individually, and even momentarily variable. The reader will still remain the active producer of meaning. The reader's voice will still be the one to give life to the story. The reader will continue to author, but will do so in a way consonant with the intentions of the research and the writing.

In a real conversation each person can interrupt the exchange, and elaborate on or correct possible misinterpretations. In a conversational exchange with the text, these safeguards against misinterpretation or misappropriation of the text are not possible. The author is absent. It becomes our role as readers, then, to temper the necessary subjectivity of our reading with attention both to the context of the writing as well as to the context of our own reading. Although readers' interpretations are formed by their own perspectives, the aim is to effect a mediation between the reading and writing perspectives. Within a reading community that understands the purpose and methodology of collaborative narrative inquiry, a dialogic process of reading follows naturally.

The rhetoric of the text invites just such a conversational commingling of the reader with the trace of the absent author, which is the text. The personal conversational tone that characterizes the writing of collaborative narrative inquiry signals a concordant reading stance for the reader. Much as a biology text suggests an efferent reading and poetry invites an aesthetic reading stance, the texts of collaborative narrative inquiry encourage a participatory stance that seeks to connect with the existence behind the text.

This is not an undue privileging of the teacher/writer's voice in the text, but a seeking to understand that voice. Neither does this reading stance pay attention to the teacher's voice as the one right voice at the expense of other voices that are also part of the classroom community. The one right reading in the New Critical sense is not our concern. A tussle between the binary opposites of right and wrong or voiced and voiceless is not at issue here. Rather, the aim is to seek connectedness through the reader's dialogical transaction with the text. In this way fidelity extends from the way in which the story was originally received and recorded to the way also in which it is read.

Reading and interpreting from a collaborative stance characterized by an attitude of caring does not preclude a critical reading of the work. Both the written and the social text can be submitted to the three levels of reading, interpretation, and criticism, as Scholes (1985) defines them. Although these are not discreet activities to be mapped in a linear progression, Scholes distinguishes them in this way: "In *reading* we produce *text within text*; in *interpreting* we produce *text upon text*; and in *criticizing* we produce *text against text*" (p. 24). Reading, the first step in the transaction with the text, involves the knowledge of the generic and cultural codes of the text. By means of these codes we are able to process the words of a literary text and the signs of a social text; we can locate and understand the characters, their situations, and their actions. We can reconstruct the world of the text and follow the narrative. Interpretation, which coincides with or follows reading, is the process of making connections between the single instances in the text and its larger cultural context. In this way interpretation gives meaning and assigns significance to what has been read. But interpretation is incomplete without further extension into criticism. Criticism is the process of moving outside the text in order to examine its function and essential effect. Criticism is not a matter of personal preference or negation. Rather, it is a process of reflecting on the text, questioning it, examining its implications, and recognizing its assertions. The purpose of criticism is to extend or reeducate the perception of a text, its subtleties and its complexities.

Eisner (1979) describes the thoughtful study of educational phenomena in a similar way, using the terms *description, interpretation*, and *evaluation* to explain the form and function of educational criticism. As a first step, description of an educational experience lets the reader feel and live the situation. But describing a situation without providing a context for understanding the whole is meaningless. As in literary theory, which moves from reading to interpretation, educational criticism moves from description to interpretation. In order to gain an understanding of what has been rendered, significant connections are made between the events in the classroom and ideas, concepts, and theories from the social sciences. Interpretation is followed by evaluation. Evaluation in Eisner's thinking is, again, not a negative appraisal, but rather an act of disclosure, an illumination of an event, so that a more meaningful appraisal can be made.

In seeking to make sense of the complexities of classroom research and the problematic issues therein, a dialogic interplay between different disciplines can push us forward in our knowing and illuminate for us some of the dark spots in our understanding. As Bateson (1990) observes, "The most creative thinking occurs at the meeting place of disciplines" (p. 75). Issues of voice, authorship, and meaning that are so central to discussions of literary theory are equally significant for our work in education. The various literary theories challenge us to relate to texts and to read them in different ways. They invite us to resist closure. We have come to understand the importance of the interpretive strategies we bring to a text, and have learned how we can transact with texts to make meaning. In our study of classrooms, of teachers, their practices, and their stories, we face a similar challenge to read and to relate in new ways. Collaborative narrative inquiry is one such new way of doing research. It redefines the relationship between researcher and researched and provides a structure for telling teachers' stories within a framework of care. It becomes our responsibility, then, to consider how we will read these stories. By repositioning ourselves in relation to the text and adopting a participatory stance, our reading becomes more consonant with the principles and methods of collaborative narrative inquiry.

I undertook the writing of this text to explore some of the ethical concerns and issues of representation that arose out of my research experiences with James and Raymond. Throughout the writing, Bertolt Brecht's (1976) words guided the manner of my telling and reminded me of the presence of the reading other:

> So you should simply make the instant stand out,
> without in the process hiding what you are making it stand out from.
> . . .
> You will show the flow of events and also the course
> of your work, permitting the spectator
> To experience this now on many levels,
>   coming from Previously and
> Merging into Afterwards . . . (p. 157)

The narrative line of this story does not lead to closure, to a problem resolved. Rather, it leads to a situation revealed, an open-ended instance that invites questioning and further dialogue on confirming ways in which we can learn through teachers' stories. It is a text to be continued. . . .

References

Atwood, M. (1985). *The handmaid's tale*. Toronto: McClelland-Bantam.

Bakhtin, M. M. (1981). *The dialogic imagination* (M. Holquist, Ed.; C. Emerson and M. Holquist, Trans.). Austin: University of Texas Press.

Barnes, D. (1976). *From communication to curriculum*. Middlesex, England: Penguin.

Barthes, R. (1968/1989). The death of the author. In D. Latimer (Ed.), *Contemporary critical theory* (pp. 53–59). New York: Harcourt Brace Jovanovich.

Barthes, R. (1977). *Image music text*. New York: Hill and Wang.

Bateson, M. C. (1990). *Composing a life*. New York: Plume.

Belenky, M., Clinchy, B., Goldberger, N., & Tarule, J. (1986). *Women's ways of knowing*. New York: Basic Books.

Bleich, D. (1975). *Readings and feelings*. Urbana, IL: National Council of Teachers of English.

Brecht, B. (1976). *Poems, part three, 1938–1956*. London: Eyre Methuen.

Briscoe, C. (1990, April). *Beliefs, metaphors and teacher change: A case study*. Paper presented at the annual meeting of the American Educational Research Association, Boston.

Britton, J. (1982). *Language and learning*. Middlesex, England: Penguin.

Britzman, D. P. (1986). Cultural myths in the making of a teacher: Biography and social structure in teacher education. *Harvard Educational Review, 56*(4), 442–455.

Brody, C., Schroeder, D., Webb, K., Schulz, R., & Richert, A. (1994, April). *Collaborative narrative inquiry: Fidelity and the ethics of caring in teacher research*. Paper presented at the annual meeting of the American Educational Research Association, New Orleans.

Bronte, C. (1847/1985). *Jane Eyre*. London: Penguin.

Bruner, J. (1990). *Acts of meaning*. Cambridge, MA: Harvard University Press.

Buber, M. (1965). *Between man and man*. New York: Macmillan.

Bullough, R. V. (1990, April). *Personal history and teaching metaphors in preservice teacher education*. Paper presented at the annual meeting of the American Educational Research Association, Boston.

Burke, K. (1950). *A rhetoric of motives*. Los Angeles: University of California Press.

Butt, R., Raymond, D., & Townsend, D. (1990, April). *Speculations on the nature and facilitation of teacher development as derived from teachers' stories*. Paper presented at the annual meeting of the American Educational Research Association, Boston.

Butt, R., Raymond, D., & Yamagishi, L. (1988). Autobiographic praxis: Studying the formation of teachers' knowledge. *Journal of Curriculum Theorizing,* 7(4), 87–164.

Clandinin, D. J. (1986). *Classroom practice: Teacher images in action.* London: Falmer Press.

Clandinin, D. J. (1994, April). *Stories: Challenging the APA style.* Paper presented at the annual meeting of the American Educational Research Association, New Orleans.

Clandinin, D. J., & Connelly, F. M. (1988). Studying teachers' knowledge of classrooms: Collaborative research ethics and the negotiation of narrative. *The Journal of Educational Thought,* 22(2A), 269–282.

Clandinin, D. J., & Connelly, F. M. (1994). Personal experience methods. In N. K. Denzin & Y. S. Lincoln (Eds.), *Handbook of qualitative research* (pp. 413–427). Thousand Oaks, CA: Sage.

Cole, A. L., & Knowles, J. G. (1993). Teacher development partner research: A focus on methods and issues. *American Educational Research Journal,* 30(3), 473–495.

Coles, R. (1989). *The call of stories: Teaching and the moral imagination.* Boston: Houghton Mifflin.

Connelly, F. M., & Clandinin, D. J. (1988). *Teachers as curriculum planners: Narratives of experience.* New York: Teachers College Press.

Connelly, F. M., & Clandinin, D. J. (1990). Stories of experience and narrative inquiry. *Educational Researcher,* 19(5), 2–14.

Cortazzi, M. (1993). *Narrative analysis.* London: Falmer Press.

Culler, J. D. (1982). *On deconstruction: Theory and criticism after structuralism.* Ithaca, NY: Cornell University Press.

Cusick, P. A. (1973). *Inside high school.* New York: Holt, Rinehart, & Winston.

Dewey, J. (1916). *Democracy and education.* New York: Macmillan.

Eco, U. (1979). *The role of the reader.* Bloomington: Indiana University Press.

Eisner, E. (1979). *The educational imagination: On the design and evaluation of school programs.* New York: Macmillan.

Eisner, E. (1984). Can educational research inform educational practice? *Phi Delta Kappan,* March, 447–452.

Eliot, T. S. (1963). *Collected poems, 1909–1962.* London: Faber and Faber.

Fish, S. (1980). *Is there a text in this class? The authority of interpretive communities.* Cambridge, MA: Harvard University Press.

Foucault, M. (1989). What is an author? In R. C. Davis & R. Schleifer (Eds.), *Contemporary literary criticism: Literary and cultural studies* (pp. 262–275). New York: Longman.

Gadamer, H. G. (1960). *Wahrheit und Methode* [Truth and Method]. Tübinger: Mohr.

Geertz, C. (1973). *The interpretation of cultures.* New York: Basic Books.

Geertz, C. (1988). *Works and lives.* Stanford, CA: Stanford University Press.

Genette, G. (1980). *Narrative discourse.* Ithaca, NY: Cornell University Press.

Grumet, M. (1987). The politics of personal knowledge. *Curriculum Inquiry,* 17(3), 319–329.

Grumet, M. (1988). *Bitter milk.* Amherst: The University of Massachusetts Press.

Harley, J. B. (1992). Deconstructing the map. In T. J. Barnes & J. S. Duncan (Eds.), *Writing worlds* (pp. 231–247). London: Routledge.

Heath, S. B. (1983). *Ways with words.* Cambridge, MA: Cambridge University Press.

Heilbrun, C. G. (1988). *Writing a woman's life.* New York: Ballantine Books.

Holland, N. (1968). *The dynamics of literary response.* New York: Oxford University Press.

Holland, N. (1975). *Five readers reading.* New Haven: Yale University Press.

Iser, W. (1978). *The act of reading: A theory of aesthetic response.* Baltimore, MD: Johns Hopkins University Press.

Jackson, P. (1968). *Life in classrooms.* New York: Teachers College Press.

Kimmel, A. J. (1989). *Ethics and values in applied social research.* Newbury Park, CA: Sage.

Knowles, J. G., & Ems, D. (1990, April). *The convergence of teacher educators' and preservice teachers' personal histories: Shaping pedagogy.* Paper presented at the annual meeting of the American Educational Research Association, Boston.

Lakoff, G., & Johnson, M. (1988). Metaphors we live by. In W. C. Booth & M. W. Gregory (Eds.), *Liberal education through reading and writing* (pp. 189–199). New York: HarperCollins.

Lester, N. B., & Onore, C. S. (1990). *Learning change.* Portsmouth, NH: Heinemann.

Lightfoot, S. L. (1983). *The good high school: Portraits of character and culture.* New York: Basic Books.

Lincoln, Y. S. (1990). Toward a categorical imperative for qualitative research. In E. Eisner & A. Peshkin (Eds.), *Qualitative inquiry in education: The continuing debate* (pp. 277–295). New York: Teachers College Press.

MacLean, M. (1986). A framework for analyzing reader-text interaction. *Journal of Research and Development in Education, 19*(2), 16–21.

Morrison, T. (1987). *Beloved.* New York: Knopf.

Noddings, N. (1984). *Caring: A feminine approach to ethics and moral education.* Berkeley: University of California Press.

Noddings, N. (1987). Fidelity in teaching, teacher education, and research for teaching. In M. Okazawa-Rey, J. Anderson, & R. Traver (Eds.), *Teachers, teaching and teacher education* (pp. 384–398). Cambridge: Harvard Educational Review.

Noddings, N. (1991). Stories in dialogue: Caring and interpersonal reasoning. In C. Witherell & N. Noddings (Eds.), *Stories lives tell: Narrative and dialogue in education* (pp. 157–170). New York: Teachers College Press.

Noddings, N. (1992). *The challenge to care in schools: An alternative approach to education.* New York: Teachers College Press.

Olson, J. K. (1980). *Innovative doctrines and practical dilemmas: A case study of curriculum translation.* Unpublished doctoral dissertation, University of Birmingham, Birmingham, England.

Pajares, M. F. (1992). Teachers' beliefs and educational research: Cleaning up a messy construct. *Review of Educational Research, 62*(3), 307–332.

Peshkin, A. (1985). Virtuous subjectivity: In the participant-observer's eyes. In

D. Berg & K. Smith (Eds.), *Exploring clinical methods for social research* (pp. 267–281). Beverly Hills, CA: Sage.

Pinar, W. (1988). Autobiography and the architecture of self. *Journal of Curriculum Theorizing, 8*(1), 7–35.

Polkinghorne, D. (1988). *Narrative knowing in the human sciences.* Albany: State University of New York Press.

Punch, M. (1994). Politics and ethics in qualitative research. In N. K. Denzin & Y. S. Lincoln (Eds.), *Handbook of qualitative research* (pp. 83–97). Thousand Oaks, CA: Sage.

Rosenblatt, L. M. (1938/1976). *Literature as exploration.* New York: Noble and Noble.

Rosenblatt, L. M. (1978). *The reader, the text, the poem.* Carbondale: Southern Illinois University Press.

Rosenblatt, L. M. (1988). *Writing and reading: The transactional theory* (Technical Report No. 13). Berkeley: University of California Center for the Study of Writing.

Rushdie, S. (1991). *Imaginary homelands.* London: Granta.

Schatzman, L., & Strauss, A. L. (1973). *Field research: Strategies for natural sociology.* Englewood Cliffs, NJ: Prentice-Hall.

Scholes, R. (1985). *Textual power.* New Haven, CT: Yale University Press.

Schweickart, P. (1989). Reading ourselves: Toward a feminist theory of reading. In R. C. Davis & R. Schleifer (Eds.), *Contemporary literary criticism: Literary and cultural studies* (pp. 118–141). New York: Longman.

Scudder, J. R. (1971). Freedom with authority: A Buber model for teaching. In R. T. Hyman (Ed.), *Contemporary thought on teaching* (pp. 197–206). Englewood Cliffs, NJ: Prentice-Hall.

Singer, I. B. (1976). *Naftali the storyteller and his horse, Sus.* New York: Farrar, Strauss & Giroux.

Smith, L. (1990). Ethics in qualitative field research: An individual perspective. In E. Eisner & A. Peshkin (Eds.), *Qualitative inquiry in education: The continuing debate* (pp. 258–276). New York: Teachers College Press.

Stenhouse, L. (1967). *Culture and education.* New York: Weybright & Talley.

Suleiman, S., & Crosman, I. (Eds.). (1980). *The reader in the text.* Princeton, NJ: Princeton University Press.

Thomas, A. (1989). *Latakia.* Vancouver: Talonbooks.

Van Manen, M. (1977). Linking ways of knowing with ways of being practical. *Curriculum Inquiry, 6,* 205–228.

Weaver, C. (1985). Parallels between new paradigms in science and in reading and literary theories: An essay review. *Research in the Teaching of English, 19*(3), 298–316.

White, H. (1978/1989). *Tropics in discourse: Essays in cultural criticism.* Baltimore: Johns Hopkins University Press.

White, M., & Epston, D. (1990). *Narrative means to therapeutic ends.* New York: W. W. Norton.

Wolcott, H. F. (1990). On seeking—and rejecting—validity in qualitative research. In E. Eisner & A. Peshkin (Eds.), *Qualitative inquiry in education: The continuing debate* (pp. 121–152). New York: Teachers College Press.

Zeichner, K., & Tabachnik, B. (1985). The development of teacher perspectives: Social strategies and institutional control in the socialization of beginning teachers. *Journal of Education for Teachers, 11,* 1–25.

About the Author

Renate Schulz is an Assistant Professor at the University of Manitoba, Canada, where she teaches Language Arts in the Teacher Education Program of the Winnipeg Education Centre. A former high school English teacher, she holds an M.Ed. from Queen's University in Kingston, Ontario, and a Ph.D. from the University of North Dakota. Dr. Schulz has been actively involved in establishing and working with elementary and secondary school teachers in school–university collaboratives. She has presented and published in the areas of language arts, teacher education, and teacher development. Most recently she was invited to work with educators in Zimbabwe to facilitate change in that country's elementary school language arts curriculum.

Index